The Legacy of Terry Fox & John Morton

Solving the Mystery on How They Met

Bruce A. Woods

FriesenPress

Suite 300 - 990 Fort St
Victoria, BC, V8V 3K2
Canada

www.friesenpress.com

Copyright © 2018 by Bruce A. Woods
First Edition — 2018

All rights reserved.

No part of this publication may be reproduced in any form, or by any means, electronic or mechanical, including photocopying, recording, or any information browsing, storage, or retrieval system, without permission in writing from FriesenPress.

ISBN
978-1-5255-2263-5 (Hardcover)
978-1-5255-2264-2 (Paperback)
978-1-5255-2265-9 (eBook)

1. BIOGRAPHY & AUTOBIOGRAPHY

Distributed to the trade by The Ingram Book Company

Table of Contents

Foreward vii
Book One 1
The Real Story of Terry Fox
    Introduction 3
    Chapter One: Rika Noda 6
    Chapter Two: The Accident 9
    Chapter Three: Romance 11
    Chapter Four: Rivalry of Love 19
    Conclusion 24
Book Two 27
The John Morton Story
    Historical Perspective on John Morton 29
    Introduction 31
    Chapter One Canada: A Forbidding Place 34
    Chapter Two The Three Greenhorns 40
    Chapter Three Childhood 46
    Chapter Four The New World 53
    Chapter Five It's an Indian World 63
    Chapter Six Faded Gold 72
    Chapter Seven The Best of Possible Worlds 76

Chapter Eight Morton's Shack 83
Chapter Nine A Renamed City Takes Off 89
Chapter Ten Canada Comes of Age 97
Chapter Eleven The Adventurer Comes Home to Find a Bride . 102
Chapter Twelve The Canadian Pacific Railroad Barons
Steal the West 112
Chapter Thirteen The Allure of Romance Never Dies 115
Chapter Fourteen England Bound 127
Chapter Fifteen Vancouver is our Home 131
Chapter Sixteen Vancouver's Taj Mahal 142
Some Final Reflections 153

Appendix One **156**
Appendix Two **158**
Appendix Three **160**
Bibliography 162
About the Author 166

Bruce and Joan Woods

TRIBUTE

I dedicate this book to the love of my life. Her inspiration and prodding made me an author of a best-selling Canadian book "Between Two Women: A Stratford Story", my autobiography. It was her idea and without her advice and help it would never have made it to press. This biography of two famous Vancouver pioneers is the bi-product. Hope you enjoy the read.

The Ruth Morton Memorial Baptist Church as it stands today

This church was built with funds provided by John Morton, Vancouver's first settler. It was the church Terry Fox occasionally attended. In an indirect way John Morton impacted the life of many Vancouver citizens. Terry Fox was one of them.

Foreward

The title of this book raises an interesting question. How can two men who lived one century apart ever meet? Or to put the issue in another format, years ago John Donne wrote those famous words, "no man is an island". In a round about way John Morton cast a shadow over Terry Fox that made a significant difference that needs to be explained [Book II].

I shall now endeavour to initiate the enigma. [Book I].

I have undertaken to write a story about two men that I greatly admire. The first is Terry Fox who needs no introduction. The second is John Morton, Vancouver's first pioneer settler. However, their stories cannot be told without reference to the women that impacted their careers. The subplot is the not-too-familiar romance story that shaped their lives, or in other words, the untold women who influenced their lives.

Book II will affirm the identification I feel for John Morton because my own life's journey one hundred years later has a few similarities. The mystery of how the paths of John Morton and Terry Fox crossed even though they never met one another is a riddle that will be revealed in the conclusion.

John Morton faced risks far beyond this author's experience yet there are similarities. He had to say goodbye to friends and family and start over in the new world. I did something analogous when I left my hometown of Stratford, Ontario. Separation brings loneliness and I know the feeling. Morton met Robert Lennie, a pastor who was a life changer for this pioneer. I know this experience as well when I became a Christian only my mentor was evangelist Barry Moore. For me to identify with John Morton is now in the arena of interpretation. The final result is the story itself – mainly history but almost a novel.

Many have said, "Bruce, you are a storyteller." I hope this account rates a similar response. The tale of Vancouver's first settler, John Morton, is the subject of Book II. Book I deals with Vancouver's most famous resident Terry Fox. My writing style follows the pattern of my earlier books, "Between Two Women, A Stratford Story" and "Between Two Worlds, A Canadian Story." They were written to entertain. I am not a historian. I make no effort to write a history book that will invite scholastic scrutiny. My writing style has been described by some as racy, even bordering on slang. I blend my imagination into the story for my readers. I do, although, include historical sidebars and incidents because, if it interests me, I believe it will interest my readers as well. That said, this book is not fiction, it is truth.

The material I give you is heavily reliant on others. Scholars will recognize Alan Morley, J.S. Mathews and J.H. Grant. The sources are sparse but I was favoured by the opportunity to interview Morton's granddaughter, Viola Gleig, while she was still alive. Far as I know, I am the only Canadian writer alive today that can say that. There are few footnotes or other devices so dear to the academician. Everything on Morton is in a single package at the Vancouver Archives. Meantime, I have woven a story to captivate the average reader. If this story inspires some to find out more, there is a bibliography at end of the book.

In this venture I am not without precedent. My Greatest Teacher used stories to captivate his audience. Those ancient tales were probably based on real life situations but enhanced in order to make a point. Storytelling trumps the exactitude of history. The Morton story really happened. I now affirm that 97% of my story is true and the rest is interpretation. On the Terry Fox story I think I could claim 99% so, I hope you will enjoy the read.

Book One

The Real Story of Terry Fox

Introduction

How the stories of an English Greenhorn (Book II) and a Canadian athlete (Book I) who are separated by a century could cross paths is now the focus of our attention. A great story of Vancouver's most famous contemporary citizen and Vancouver's first settler requires an explanation. Let us begin with the hero everybody knows by the name of Terry Fox. Sure—lots of people fall in love and have nothing to do with church, but I affirm—they do so at their loss. Next question! How did church life affect the experience that put our hero into the path of a Japanese girl by the name of Rika Noda? Our amazing story has now just begun.

The only church Terry Fox ever attended was the Ruth Morton Memorial Baptist Church in 1979 and 1980 and that happened only a few times. In this he was one better than John Morton the Christian benefactor and pioneer, because Morton died before the church he financed was ever built. Dare we call anybody a Christian who in one short lifetime went to church about a half a dozen times. This kind of affirmation demands some evidence. The balance of our narrative will provide the testimony. Before we reveal the proof, our story will relate a unique and unimaginable sequence of events.

The first formidable hurdle was the collision of nationalities, language and culture spread apart by ten thousand miles. Throw in a little bit of history with the impossible roadblock of two people with temperaments dramatically opposed to one another and we have the setting for the Christian conversion of an agnostic by the name of Terry Fox.

When one has a story to tell we must look for origins, so first we start with Terry. Born on July 28, 1958, Terry Fox entered this world in Winnipeg, the second son of Rolland and Betty Fox. Rolly Fox was a switchman working for the Canadian National Railway; eventually Rolly and Betty would have four children. At the age of twelve, Terry was informed by his parents that they were moving to British Columbia and Port Coquitlam became the ideal place for the Fox kids to grow up. The roll call reads as follows, Fred, the oldest, Terry, Darrell and Judith. For Terry, there was roughhousing with his father and brothers. Next came summer jobs picking blueberries, saving the money to buy his own clothes, a bike or school supplies. There were quiet times as well, when he would play alone for hours. School meant more than hard work: it meant new friends. One boy, Doug Alward, began a friendship with Terry that would endure for a shorter lifetime than we could have wished for. Coincidence or design? Doug Alward was a young Christian man who with a quiet temperament rarely ever talked about his faith but chose to live it instead; ultimately he would become Terry's best friend. Eventually they would wind up together on Terry's Marathon of Hope. That's when they discovered that when two friends have to live together for half a year in a small trailer there will be plenty of arguments that never occurred before. Terry's personality was aggressive, Doug tended to introvert when he objected to mettlesome comments, which explains why these two guys got along so well.

And there were sports!

Terry played soccer, baseball and rugby. He competed in track and field and took up cross country running, but what he wanted to do more than anything else was to play basketball. At first Terry wasn't very good at the game, but he wouldn't give up his dreams. All through the summer before grade nine, he played one-on-one with Doug. That fall, Terry ran to school each morning and stayed late after classes so he could practice. The Fox stubbornness paid off. By grade ten. Terry had earned a place on the basketball team. Two years later when he and Doug graduated, they shared the *Athlete of the Year Award*. His heart set on a good education, Terry enrolled at Simon Fraser University, and, more competitive than ever, made the basketball team.

He had plans. Eventually he hoped to become a high school Phys Ed teacher. His future looked bright. Life was good.[1] Most young men have dreams of meeting the girl of their dreams and Terry was no exception—so let's meet the young lady destined to fulfill this role.

---

1 This account is from *Terry Fox: A Story of Hope* by Maxine Trottier

Chapter One:
Rika Noda

How does the daughter of a Japanese Buddhist family wind off attending the Ruth Morton Memorial Baptist Church Sunday School and eventually become a committed Christian. Our story begins with George Kitchen, an electrician who on Sundays drove a bus to pick up children in and around Central Vancouver for Sunday School. In the process of time in the year 1966, he made a visit to a house on the corner of 23rd and Fraser Street and met Misaho and Akiko Noda. Misaho was Japanese and had come to Canada seeking his fortune by fishing for salmon off the British Columbia coast. Misaho was a hard worker and despite many trials succeeded in his endeavour.

Roll the clock back (from 1966) twenty-five years to December 7th, 1941. Remember World War II and the advent of the Pearl Harbour disaster. That's when the United States and Canada declared war on Japan. One Japanese immigrant was asked the question, "Whose side are you on?" His reply was interesting. "When your mother and your father have a fight, whose side do you pick?" Like our American counterparts Canada wasn't interested in an answer. Misaho wasn't even given a choice. A Canadian Army officer showed up at his door one day to inform him that he was an alien. Next, his fishing boat was confiscated and sold, Misaho was placed in an internment camp in

Ontario, one of the most ignominious decisions the Canadian government made during those tumultuous years.

After war's end, Misaho returned to Vancouver, raised the money and returned to what he knew best—fishing. By family arrangement and a little bit of romance, he was introduced to his Japanese bride and Akiko became his wife. Gradually he rebuilt his fishing business. Many years later, after an official government apology, he was compensated with a check for $26,000. Of course, considering inflation, the money was a fraction of his original loss. It was the apology that really mattered.

Fast forward again to the year 1966, Rika and her older sister Alisa were in a weekly Buddhist class taught in Japanese and couldn't understand a word. When George Kitchen knocked at the Noda door, Akiko with her children's welfare in mind had an idea. An English-speaking Sunday School four blocks away—hymmm! Mother Noda considered George Kitchen's offer and decided it would be a good idea for her daughters, because this way they could learn Canadian ways. At this point Alisa the elder daughter was eleven years old and Rika was eight.

However with newfound prosperity, the Noda's bought a house on Elliott Street just four doors from Marine Drive, four and a half miles from church. Suddenly the girls could no longer attend the Ruth Morton Memorial Baptist Sunday School and Mr. Noda had no intention of providing Sunday transportation. The consternation of angels in heaven over this precarious crises was resolved when Rev. Bruce Woods (Yah, that's me) the newly called church pastor bought a house five doors south of the Nodas, a little below Marine Drive overlooking the Fraser River. Problem solved! Every Sunday with our family of six we called at the Noda house and packed Rika and Alisa on top of our three children in the back seat. Our youngest still a baby sat in the front. (These were the days before seat belts and the laws that enforced them). Our daughter Debbie and Alisa were the same age and soon became fast friends. Friends—at least except when they debated Christianity. Alisa was still a Buddhist. Then one the day the miracle happened and Alisa became a Christian. From that time onwards Alisa and our daughter Debbie Woods not only shared the same school (David Oppenheimer) but they also shared their faith. Meantime Rika Noda who watched and listened was fascinated by all this and soon followed her sister's decision. A few years later she was baptized by my successor the Rev. Don Merritt and joined the church. My memory of Rika was always how quiet her personality seemed to be. Little did I understand the depth of her commitment. In 1972, I moved to Hamilton, Ontario for our next ministry and would not meet Rika again for another twelve years.

In due time Rika would become the pastor of youth at the Ruth Morton Memorial church. I would have been pleasantly surprised had I known that Rika would one day lead the young people of that very special church. In addition, with her musical skills she was involved in the worship program, but now I'm getting ahead of my story.

This multitalented girl would excel in other pursuits as well. But first let's go back to 1979. Freshly graduated from Langara College, with a diploma in Recreational Leadership, Rika wanted to do something for *persons in need*. That's when she met Tim Frick who worked with handicapped athletes. Desiring to show her Christian testimony in practical ways she got involved with Frick's Wheelchair Basketball Tournaments. Next came some very special events, which would capture a nation's attention. Like most of my readers I was unaware of these things, which I now relate. So how did I find out about the hidden story of Terry Fox.

In 1984 Rika paid us a visit in Hamilton, Ontario three years after Terry Fox had died staying with us for a week. What she had to share with us was riveting to say the least, especially with her disclosures about who the famous Terry Fox really was compared to what the public imagines they know.

Chapter Two:
The Accident

In 1976, Terry was now an eighteen-year old teenager with a future. One day driving home in the rain distracted by a moment's diversion he had an accident on a bridge just outside of his hometown, Port Coquitlam. The incident coincided with an ominous medical crises revealed at the same time—a lethal case of bone cancer. How an athletic teenager could have cancer was the inexplicable mystery of his life. Good at sports and determined to succeed Terry wondered, "Was this accident the thing that caused so much pain in his knee? With an X-ray and a bone scan the verdict revealed the unthinkable. Terry Fox had bone cancer. Terry wondered if the accident had anything to do with it. His doctors said no but informed him that his leg would have to be amputated as soon as possible. Maxine Trottier picks up the story from here.

"At first, he cried at the thought of what had happened, at what faced him, but Terry pulled himself together. This was just one more challenge. He had worked hard before to achieve his goals and he could do it again, even if it meant doing it with only one leg. He wouldn't let anyone pity him, any more than he would pity himself.

Terry's fight with cancer had begun.

Six days later, his leg was amputated and within a few incredible weeks, he was learning to walk wearing a temporary prosthesis. One can only speculate how this affected a mother's love for her child but to be sure from this time on the relationship deepened greatly. Meantime, Terry began chemotherapy at the cancer clinic. For Terry, those were difficult months. The suffering he saw at the cancer clinic moved him deeply. When his treatment was finished, Terry left the hospital a changed person. He believed that he now had a debt to pay, that he would live his life to give courage to people who had been stricken by cancer. The night before his surgery, he had read about an amputee runner, a man who had run the New York City Marathon. It had filled him not only with admiration, but with hope. He now had a new dream, that for the time being he kept to himself.

A few years earlier a guy by the name of Rick Hansen had a back injury/accident that immobilized him confining him to a wheel chair. Alike in nature to Terry Fox, he wanted to participate with others with similar problems. Hansen and Fox met and were involved with a wheelchair basketball team which took them through adventures that can be read about in the book that Hanson wrote.[2]

So at this point Terry Fox and Rick had met with one thing in common, they both needed a wheelchair scooter when it came to playing basketball. Rick was the central figure for the Canadian Wheelchair Sports Association. Together this pair of athletes with their teammates won the National Championship staged in Edmonton in 1977. They would go on with others to win two more. You can't win a championship without practice and Rick Hanson needed some help from somebody who was able bodied—so that's where Tim Frick entered the picture. Tim had a passion to help the handicapped and he still does so to this day. Needing a little help, he had an applicant whose name was Rika Noda and hired her on the spot. That's how Rika Noda and Terry Fox first met.

---

2 Rick: *The Rick Hanson Story*, Trade Paperbacks, Indigo Books and Music

Chapter Three:
Romance

Somebody said it long ago, what makes the world go round is romance—romance—romance. What the public doesn't know is that Terry Fox had a girlfriend who has quite a story all by itself and she's not talking about it although she knows I'm going to spill the beans. Let me introduce you to the girl of Terry Fox's dreams. Rika Noda—and she had a passion to help the handicapped. With this in mind she had decided to help out with a mentally retarded young man with the mentality of a two year old. I tell you this to give you some idea of her Christian compassion. Looking for a wider world where she could make a contribution she thought about the physically handicapped. Providentially she met Tim Frick who invited her to help out at volleyball and basketball practices for the handicapped. As already explained, it was here that Rika first met Terry Fox. My mental image of Terry Fox is a strongman over six feet tall. Strongman he was but really not too different from the average nineteen-year old. In actual fact Terry was five foot ten, which makes him just about the same as most of us, give or take a few inches.

Rika was a pretty girl that we might call petite. At first it was just a casual conversation. Aha! Let's face it, we were made for romance—and marriage is the by-product. Next it was a date. Terry consulted with Rick Hansen who suggested, "Why don't you take her to the

Sears Revolving Restaurant, that's a nice place." Rika responded with a satisfying yes and suddenly Betty Fox had a competitor for Terry's affection. After that a very interesting life style between two very unusual lovers began to unfold. In the summer of 1977 romance bloomed, but there was an issue. As a Christian, Rika was facing a problem. Terry didn't believe in God and if there was a God—well, for Terry—he just didn't know and that's when he revealed himself to be an agnostic.

Would Rika be willing to marry an agnostic was the next question. When Terry Fox discovered the answer was no, he challenged Rika— Okay, convince me! When you love somebody (and Rika and Terry had both been smitten by romance) what do you do? Rika's solution was to give him an unusual book to read. It was not the ordinary kind. *The Hobbit* written by J.R.R. Tolkien many years before Terry and Rika had met, is a fantasy book with no allusions to Christianity, but designed to raise the eternal questions. Rika had noticed that Terry had a bright mind, so she put him to the test. Tolkien wrote his fairy tale books with the idea of setting up the subconscious to investigate the supernatural. In other words, evangelism by a subtle appeal to a thinking mind; especially when it comes to the eternal issues. Some people take their handicaps with a benign acceptance but Rika had noticed that Terry couldn't help but ask the searching questions including—why me?

Understandingly, Terry was a conflicted personality who couldn't accept the loss of his leg through cancer. How to tame an angry boyfriend became Rika's next challenge. Solution—books! For starters and admittedly with her Christian faith in mind is why she had recommended J.R.R. Tolkien's *The Hobbit*. Terry was intrigued by Tolkien and was soon reading the three volume *Lord of the Rings*. Tolkien has two kinds of readers, those who are fascinated by philosophical fantasy and those who look beyond the fantasy to things eternal. Eighty years ago, Tolkien engaged C.S. Lewis an avowed atheist on this very kind of Christian mythology. After Lewis returned in 1936 from a visit to Soviet Russia this scholastic atheist had been shaken by his disillusionment with Communism. Debating with Tolkien, Owen Barfield and Charles Williams who called their club the Inklings, Lewis began to reconsider the Christianity he had rejected and ultimately, thanks mainly to Tolkien became a Christian. Tolkien believed that mythology was a way to undermine atheism, which ultimately led him to write his world famous trilogy *Lord of the Rings* to which we have already alluded. As Tolkien debated Lewis on Christianity, not only did he win a new convert, but he inspired Lewis to write the world famous *The Lion, the Witch and the Wardrobe* which carries Christian mythology even further. Tolkien and Lewis became soul mates writing to challenge their readers to examine Christianity with far reaching results including sceptics all the way from Zanzibar to Vancouver.

It was this kind of reasoning that led Rika to stimulate the thinking of Terry Fox because Rika knew that behind that feisty façade was a brain in search of answers to philosophical questions. It is in this kind of benevolence those who have lived and died before us create a legacy which affects us all. In other words, thanks to Rika, Terry discovered in-depth reading from authors who even though no longer alive they still impact a future generation. Next Rika would take Terry Fox to the eternal issues of life and death challenging him to embrace Christianity. Ultimately Fox read everything Tolkien ever wrote including the "Silmarillion" which explains why Tolkien this world-famous author wrote his books. Tolkien the Christian wanted his readers to face the issues of life and the question of what happens to us after death. Most people enjoy his books and conclude—what a great fairy-tale, others look deeper and embrace the faith that the New Testament describes, especially for anyone willing to examine the evidence. Terry did just that and with Rika's help, after reading the Bible for himself, became a believer. He even went to church a few times with Rika. So where did they go—naturally—Rika's church, Ruth Morton Memorial Baptist, home of the magnificent memorial stain glass window that celebrates John Morton's love for his beloved Ruth.

Now Terry Fox stands in contrast with the rest of his family, because as far as I know the Fox family like most people these days was not a member of any church. Darrell Fox remembers that Betty had sent her kids to a Sunday School for a brief time during their Winnipeg days but can't remember what church it was. What kind of discussions this might have led to with his kith and kin nobody knows, but understanding Terry's feisty nature there must have been some interesting family conversations.

Simultaneous with these character-shaping experiences, Terry's vision for a cancer fundraiser was taking shape. Terry Fox had a vision. Today, the Marathon of Hope is history but in 1978 it was still only a dream in Terry's mind. The other vexing question was would Terry and Rika get married before or after the run? Remember! For Rika the vital question had been—Terry Fox are you willing to become a follower of Jesus Christ! But now that the first hurdle was crossed, there were some other issues. In other words at this point, if a marriage was in the works, it would have to be postponed. This and other issues will be explained later. The Marathon of Hope came first.

After that incredible and tumultuous Marathon of Hope, which prevented a premature marriage came a great deal of suffering and death. Time heals the wounds of tragedy. East revisits the West. After four years, came an invitation from a newspaper reporter by the name of Charles Wilkinson who worked for the Hamilton Spectator. Regarding Christianity Wilkinson asked Rika this searching question, "Did he say this (his Christianity) to please you?" Rika's answer was unequivocal.

"No, he would never do anything like that to please someone else. He was extremely strong-willed. He had his own mind. He would feel phony if he made a decision in that way—and he was the most un-phony person I have ever met. He was very, very honest. In fact, during his Marathon of Hope run, when he stopped for the night, he would touch a post. The next morning, he would go back to that post and touch it again, and start exactly where he had left off. He said once. "If I don't do that, people wouldn't trust me any more." For Terry Fox, telling the truth was crucial.

Miss Noda said that when Terry Fox first became a Christian, he read the Bible practically every night. "I seem to remember him saying he finished it in a comparatively short time. He was very interested, and wanted to know more. I think he put some of us older Christians to shame in the way he studied the Bible so diligently.

"When he started training for the run, his time for Bible reading became much shorter. He became very tired and very grumpy." (I have to interject something here. The original Marathon story originates in Greece where the Greeks defeated the invading Persian Army in 490 BC. To deliver the happy news an athlete by the name of Pheidippides who ran the 42 kilometers (26 miles) from Marathon to Athens with the joyful news of a Greek victory enters our picture. One does not run 42 kilometers every day without training. This was the challenge Terry Fox wanted to prepare for and very time consuming for someone contemplating marriage).

Wilkinson next asked, "Was he having much pain then?" Rika's reply was, "He could tolerate a lot of pain especially on his run. As for the Bible, he didn't lose interest. It was just that he gained another interest, another priority, and he was training all day long—just training, sleeping; then all the promotion, trying to get sponsors, and then he went on the run. I kept in touch with him on the Marathon. His friend, Doug Alward, who was with him, told me that Terry's testimony was not very clear on the run. Sometimes it seemed as though he was angry with God, or defying God. He went through the same thing that I had done, but he had more reason to act this way."

Terry would get up at five o'clock to run, and during the day he would give interviews, and speak once or twice at various places. One of the newspapers wanted him to check in at certain points, and he would have to go and find a phone booth.[3] (Remember, this was the time before cell phones and the I-pad).

Evidence! I could have related all the above because Rika had shared it with us when she stayed with us on her visit to Hamilton thirty-three years ago. I have quoted Wilkerson so that my readers will not be wondering if I have exaggerated the story. So let us continue. The graphic news of this incredible run would eventually introduce Terry Fox to Prime Minister Pierre Elliott Trudeau in Ottawa plus any number of notable and famous people. The unknown story is that when Terry was in need of inspiration and support during his cross Canada run, to the frustration of his mother, it was to Rika that he would phone first and then his mother. When his heroic run ended in northern Ontario, he once again sought out Rika. It's not that Terry didn't love his mother and his family, it's just that Terry also had a romantic nature which manifested itself in his affection for Rika. The normal relationships with parents and family did not exclude a girl friend for encouragement.

Terry Fox never got the opportunity to attend church very much, but he sure made an impression when he attended Ruth Morton just once after his famous run. From that time on, Terry languished in a hospital till he died.

There is a message here for all of us. We were made for romance and marriage is the illustration. But—for all of the shortcomings of marriage (because what we get is never perfect) marriage is still the earthly ultimate until something better comes along but that takes death. That's when we meet the author of love who is none other than God Himself. Unlike most of us Terry's introduction came sooner than he had originally anticipated.

The story of Rick Hansen who picked up the fallen torch and circled the globe has been told elsewhere. He too is one of Rika's friends.

---

3   Charles Wilkinson, The Hamilton Spectator, Saturday, October 6, 1984

Time to pause and reminisce on those courtship days, when two young people had discovered romance. Rika tells an amusing story of her days with Terry before he became so famous: "...like the time I (Rika) participated in one of the wheelchair marathons (coaches often participated to encourage the athletes) and everyone thought I was disabled. When I wheeled into the stadium (of course I had to be last) they gave me a standing ovation, another coach who was running beside me whispered 'whatever you do, don't get out of that chair!' Too funny! I still laugh about that." That was in the early days, meantime Terry and Rika had become boyfriend and girlfriend—they were very close. Later Wilkinson would ask, "Would you have married Terry if he had gone on to live?" Rika's answer is interesting, "It's hard to say." She replied. "We talked a lot about marriage, but he had always wanted to run, and it came to the point where we had to discontinue the relationship. I still saw him often, but not as girlfriend. He just felt it wasn't fair to me because of all his training time. So he continued training for his Marathon of Hope to run across Canada and I continued to help him. That was a high priority for him. I think we could have continued our relationship, but I wondered how important it was to him at that point. I was willing to be around and help him. I wasn't going to complain if he couldn't take me out to dinner or a movie. I was ready to give everything I had, too. It didn't seem that he understood what a strong relationship could be, even though at times marriage was a very good possibility in the future. But I wasn't totally at peace with it, because of his attitude towards different things.

"He was very, very stubborn , and I thought. 'Can you live with this stubborn person?' I was a little bit stubborn, too."

So along with my readers I think it is reasonable to acknowledge that romance had flowered, but had to be postponed for a while.

The world soon forgets the people that impact others for the greater good. Rika is one of those illustrious people and joins the cavalcade of so many who have been part of the congregation of the

Ruth Morton Memorial Baptist Church to be a blessing to the world. If one were to examine the records they include a long list of professionals in business as well as in Christian mission.

When Terry Fox returned to Vancouver, it unfortunately was downhill after that. With today's medical technology, Terry Fox might have lived another fifteen years. Sadly, for Terry, death arrived all too soon.

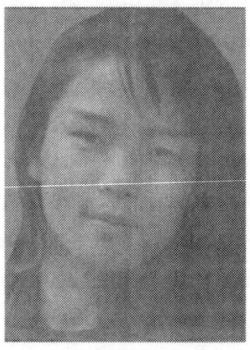

Rika Noda 1984

Chapter Four:
Rivalry of Love

Every man and woman that was born is destined to love and be loved. Sadly not everyone gets the privilege. Hopefully as a baby a mother's love comes first. Like every mother that gave birth to a baby Betty Fox loved her son. Like every mother that sees that son grow up, there comes that time when a competitor enters the scene. Rika Noda was that competitor. When two people are smitten by romance, mothers beware, marriage is part of the discussion. For both Rika and Terry it was a mutual and first time experience. During this period again to quote Rika, "Terry said that I was his first girlfriend and I was quite happy about that. We had a very, very good relationship. We were very, very close. He told me everything. He told me things that he said he wouldn't tell anybody else. He would never talk about the cancer clinic where he had chemotherapy, except to me. He would go into all kinds of detail. I guess he felt that I understood, and it helped him. The clinic was a horrible experience for him. Had it not been for Terry's passion to run the Marathon of Hope despite a premature death, Betty Fox might have played that reluctant role—Mother of the Groom. After a lifetime of ministry I can smile about a few marriages that I have conducted where a bride and a mother-in-law might have clashed. In Betty Fox's case she had a greater trial to face. The son she loved so dearly was in the icy grip of cancer.

As already explained, carrying on a courtship when one is training every day for a Marathon run proved difficult. After nine months, Rika and Terry agreed to call things off for a while even though they continued to see each other on almost a daily basis.

Eventually, the day approached for the Marathon and Terry proposed a solution. "Come on the run and afterwards we can get married, after all Doug Alward will be there as a third party." At first Rika was warm to the idea but after talking it over with her pastor, wisely Don Merritt pointed out how the press would attack that arrangement. To Terry's disappointment Rika declined the offer but plunged in to help the cause.

With corporate giants in mind Rika helped write Terry's appeal for support, which included a letter, part of which reads,

> "I was rudely awakened by the feelings that surrounded and coursed through the cancer clinic...
> ..I could not leave knowing these faces and feelings would still exist. Somewhere the hurting must stop...and I was determined to take myself to the limit for this cause.
>
> "I feel strong not only physically, but more important, emotionally. Soon I will be adding one full mile a week, and coupled with weight training I have been doing, by next April I will be ready to achieve something that for me was once only a distant dream reserved for the world of miracles – to run across Canada to raise money for the fight against cancer.
>
> "The running I can do, even if I have to crawl every last mile. We need your help. The people in cancer

clinics all over the world need people who believe in miracles.

Terry Fox. October 1979

Ultimately, Terry and Doug Alward would go it alone without Rika. Ford motor company provided the van. Imperial Oil would provide the fuel and Adidas would provide the shoes. Other companies chipped in for food and needs. The Marathon race began April 12, 1980. Meantime, Terry might write a postcard to his mother but to her chagrin, she would have to share the affection with competitor Rika Noda. Needless to say at the price we used to pay to Bell Telephone for long distance, phone calls to Rika were longer than the abbreviated phone calls to mother.

The horrific medical data that overshadowed a hero's mind could not be repressed indefinitely. Terry knew the survival rate of the bone cancer afflicted was only fifteen percent. Terry had vowed to himself that he would be one of them. I suppose it was this kind of optimism that drove him to run twenty-six miles per day. His endurance of pain and blood was the price he would pay despite the agony that only a Terry Fox would endure. Sadly the grim reality had come home to rest, Terry just might be one of the 85% who succumb. It was nothing short of a miracle that Terry even made the five thousand kilometers to Thunder Bay, Ontario. It is at this dramatic moment in our story my lifetime observation must now be made. For all mankind if we wish to be a benefit, it is crucial to discover the importance of weakness. More on this to come.

After the abrupt ending of Terry's run at Ontario's far West, he wanted to attend church once more but that could not be accomplished until after he went into hospital for four weeks. Needless to say with all the publicity the press had given him, his attendance at Rika's church created quite a stir in the congregation. One can only guess just what Terry might have been thinking, but when with Rika, he attended the Ruth Morton Memorial Baptist Church, it is an understatement to declare that as a couple they certainly created a day to remember.

Hidden from celebrative eyes, Rika suspected the worse and so did Terry, but if one is going to be optimistic and hope for recovery those thoughts will remain unspoken. It is at times like these that our Christian faith is so comforting. Terry had already informed Rika that the cancer had spread through his lungs. Not exactly material for a comforting conversation. On that and other occasions, they parted dreading the inevitable, but Terry never gave up hope. In fact he told Rika, when I get better I'm going to tell the world, I am a follower of Jesus Christ and it was God that gave me the strength to at least make it half-way.

To Betty Fox's chagrin, Terry wanted to converse with Rika whenever the opportunity arose. On one occasion following his initial release, Rika invited Terry for dinner because she knew how much he loved Akiko's Noda's cooking. As the family expected, Rika's mother had compliments on that special occasion. Terry said, "In hospital I would just pick at my food, this meal is so delicious I can stuff myself full." A few movies together and the occasional conversation between Terry and Rika was about all these two devoted friends could manage. Meantime, Mrs. Noda's savoury food could not forestall the inevitable. In the last two months of Terry's life, runaway cancer did its inevitable work.

For a solicitous press Betty and Rolland Fox had no choice. The time had come for Terry's parents to give a press conference at the Royal Columbian Hospital, in New Westminister. Maxine Trottier writes, "The nation was stunned. With incredible strength Terry had run 3,339 miles in just 143 days, and it all seemed so unfair. Sadly I think we all know that cancer has nothing to do with fairness. Terry Fox knew that what was happening to him could happen to anyone, and that now—a few more people would understand exactly what having cancer can mean. Terry had done his best to run across

Canada; he would do his best to fight this cancer and God willing, some day return to finish the run. Of course, that day never came but what a legacy! Thanks to Terry Fox seven hundred millions dollars has been raised for cancer research.

Next came the inexplicable mystery—with Terry confined to hospital, Betty Fox would allow no visitors except the immediate family. Her son was dying and he would receive the exclusive mother's love that only a mother understands.

When Rika Noda went to visit Terry Fox, she was informed—no visitors allowed. Terry languished with family and no one else was permitted without Betty's approval. One notable exception provided a press release from the Vancouver Province Newspaper. A reporter was able to tell the world that Terry Fox received comfort reading his New Testament. After that it was Rolly, his father, his mother, Betty, and his brothers, Fred and Darrell and sister, Judith. A few months earlier, when Terry had a brief brush with impending death, he himself had said, "If I really believe, and if God is really there, then I'm not going to lose even if I die."

His death was announced with an epitaph to remember. "Terry Fox had a dream." Recalled Blair MacKenzie, executive director of the British Columbia division of the Canadian Cancer Society. "That dream now belongs to everyone. We cannot and will not fail him."

Conclusion

Excluded from family decisions, Rika discovered the funeral of her beloved Terry would take place in a church close to home at Port Coquitlam. Appropriate enough I suppose because at this point that's where the Fox family lived even if they were non-church attenders. As for Terry Fox the family knew about his Christian faith but chalked that up to his friendship with Rika Noda. Cognitive Dissidence! Doug Alward and Rika Noda knew that his faith was real because that side of Terry Fox had been thoroughly discussed.

As an act of worship he only went to church a half a dozen times in his entire lifetime and that church was the Ruth Morton Memorial Baptist Church. His Christian journey had taken time but the decision to become of follower of Jesus Christ was real. So why didn't Terry Fox talk more about his newfound faith? This author can only speculate but remembering my own shaky beginnings in the faith melodrama, I think I can understand. Twenty-four hours later after Terry Fox had died, the Toronto Star picked up the story and in the June 29, 1981 issue wrote these words.

"It was decided by his doctors that Terry should have dignity in his death, as he did in life." Explained Dr. Ladislaw Antonik, the hospital's medical director.

"I don't think he shook his fist at heaven. He didn't challenge death. I think he knew he was going to die, but he simply carried on."

The Toronto Star didn't consult with Rika Noda, but the Hamilton Spectator did (albeit it was three years later). Here's what appeared in the October 6, 1984 edition,

"Miss Noda sighed, "I didn't get to see him much in the end, a couple of months before he died, it was family only, when he was in hospital. I wondered during those two months how he was doing, whether he was feeling lost, whether he (was) feeling that God was failing him, and what was going though his mind.

Naturally Rika attended the funeral of Terry Fox. After it concluded she thought it appropriate to give a word of comfort to Betty Fox, saying "At long last Terry is with the Lord to whom he belongs."

"No! That's not true! My son belongs only to me!" was her feisty reply.

Minutes later the hospital nurse took Rika aside. Knowing how Rika was feeling, she informed her that she was a Christian, and said, "I just wanted you to know that Terry was very much at peace when he died. And he said, 'I'm ready to go now. I'm ready.'" Three years later, reporter Wilkinson asked Rika this question, "Did his contact with Christianity and his Bible help a lot in that regard? To which Rika replied,

"Oh definitely! He phoned me once and said, 'If I get back,— and he wasn't sure that he could make it back, (Terry hoping for a miracle wanted to finish the race he had begun) he had told me before he left—I'm going to tell everyone it was God who helped me all the way to come across, because I could not have done it without him."

After Terry Fox had died with the funeral over, Rika Noda, Doug Alward and Darrell Fox were having coffee together to reminisce when finally Darrell posed a puzzling question, "You guys had two months to pay my brother a visit while he was in hospital, why didn't you come to see Terry in hospital?" Astonished, when Darrell found out the reason, he stammered that he had not known about his mother's decree. The Fox family is definitely one of a kind. In those days, Betty lived her life through her famous son and suffered no intruders as far as she could impose limits. Naturally Terry Fox made his own decisions regarding friends and especially for Rika Noda. In the few months before he was incapacitated by cancer as already related, from time to time, he continued to see the one he dearly esteemed on a few more occasions. I suppose in part, a mother's exclusive love for a famous son explains a few things. As for the sub-heroic three, Doug Alward, Darrell Fox and Rika, if there was some sort of impasse, they must have understood, because today they are the best of friends.

The Terry Fox foundation is now three decades in progress and has done much for cancer research. It is now under the able direction of Darrell Fox, a man with impeccable credentials. Darrell took his brother's loss with deep sorrow and many questions. Compensation for this kind of sorrow comes hard. Looking for a place to vent his grief, Darrell became a biking phenomenon. He acquired a passion for cycling and mastered his craft. In no time he was one of Canada's best.

A footnote to his accomplishments is in order. Darrell acquired a top-of-the-line bicycle for $7,000.00. Unfortunately his pride and joy caught the eye of a drug addict who was looking for a quick fix. His stolen bicycle showed up for sale a few months later in a second-hand bicycle shop. Price, sixty dollars! A Christian pastor from Port Coquitlam spotted the bike and recognizing an unprecedented bargain so he bought it. Well, it didn't take long for him to be troubled with an uneasy conscience. He soon concluded, "This must be a bicycle that has been stolen."

He phoned the police and described the bicycle to the officer, who shortly informed the pastor that the bicycle resembled one they were looking for belonging to Darrell Fox. The next day Darrell Fox got his bicycle back.

Book Two

The John Morton Story

Historical Perspective
on John Morton

Birth		1832	Reform Bills pass in England
Age	3	1837	Rebellion in Upper and Lower Canada
	7	1841	China cedes Hong Kong to Britain
	14	1848	Durham Report recommends Canadian Democracy
	16	1850	California joins the Union of American States
	25	1859	Oregon joins the Union of American States
	28	1862	USA Civil War effects, the train to Texas
		1862	Morton preempts Vancouver's West End
	33	1867	Confederation under PM Macdonald
	37	1871	British Columbia joins Confederation
	44	1878	Morton marries Jane Ann Bailey
	47	1881	Morton is a Widower with two children

49	1883	Northern Pacific RR completed to Seattle
50	1884	Morton marries Ruth Mount
51	1885	North West Rebellion under Louis Riel
52	1886	CPR railroad comes to British Columbia Hockey becomes Canada's National Sport
55	1889	Morton moves from Mission to Vancouver
56	1890	Mormon Dissenters settle at Bountiful, B.C.
58	1892	Thomas Edison patents two-way telegraph
59	1893	United States annexes Hawaii
61	1895	Russia exiles Doukhobors to Canada
71	1905	Alberta joins Confederation
73	1907	Anti Asian Vancouver Riot
75	1909	Labourer's wage in BC is 22 cents per hour
77	1911	Laurier's Liberals lose the reciprocity vote
78	1912	Morton funds the building of a church that will impact the life of others

Observation: Terry Fox and John Morton had a significant contribution to make. Both died having never known the impact their lives would make on millions of Canadians. Maybe we might even add the words, "To the World."

Introduction

City Hall was Vancouver's Golden Jubilee project. Built in art deco style, it was architect Fred Townley's masterpiece, and attracted some very special visitors including Sir Percy Vincent, Lord Mayor of London, England. There were others from afar, but what about closer to home? There were two men who conspired to bring a special visitor who embraced the nostalgic past to the fabulous future. The conspirators were Major J.S. Matthews, city archivist, and alderman J.W.Cornett. The question was simply this: is there anybody alive who had seen the city when it was first founded and had witnessed its growth to the present 350,000 inhabitants? The smile on Matthews' face belied his intent. He already knew whom he had in mind.

Ruth (Mount) Morton arrived at the city in 1884 when Vancouver was a shantytown of less than four hundred inhabitants. Fifty-three years later and at age eighty-nine, she was living in a metropolis of 350,000. A few scant blocks away from City Hall, her apartment was modest considering her means. Fame? She was the widow of Vancouver's first settler, John Morton. Credentials? In 1937, Ruth Morton was the sole remaining pioneer who had been around to see Vancouver in its infancy and was still active in a city that had become a port of call for the world. After Matthews had explained the mission to Mayor George Clark Miller, he immediately joined the conspiracy. The special event would take place Wednesday, September 8, 1937.

Alderman Cornett was given the mayor's car to pick up this doughty lady promptly at 2 P.M. Major Matthews accompanied him and together they brought Vancouver's living legend to the jewel in the crown— Vancouver's new City Hall. Ushered into the posh city council chamber, they seated the diminutive lady in the Mayor's chair (she was scarcely five feet tall) while Cornett, on behalf of Mayor Miller, placed the official gold chain around her neck and proclaimed her Vancouver's "grand madame." Her oft-quoted response was, "I think Vancouver is the nicest place on earth." Having seen City Hall and as Shakespeare has written, "rich in eye," her esteemed pair of chauffeurs, decidedly pleased with themselves, drove her back to the Montrose Apartments 1190 West Twelfth. They were not the first to honour this distinguished lady. She had a way of leaving a lasting impression on all those who met her. It is this author's privilege to continue the tradition and relate to his readers the remarkable Ruth Morton and her distinguished husband, who owns the title of Vancouver's first settler.

When one makes a claim such as "first settler," one risks a challenge for sure. We know there was an Indian village (Well—I mean an indigenous people's village) where now stands "Lumberman's Arch," however for modern history and the arrival of the white man, Morton has no real competitors. This author has therefore set forth the claim that the honour of "first settler" for Vancouver goes to John Morton. Robert Burnaby contested Morton in court that he was the first, and earned from Judge Brew the moniker of "liar or a knave." Others could claim on behalf of the first nations and cite Chief Capilano as the deserving recipient. Obviously the first nations were here long before the arrival of the white man, (approximately 82,000 of them in 1862) but for the most part they left the forest-clad peninsula (Vancouver's west end) exactly as they found it. So what about the early explorers like Captain George Vancouver? Still others might speak of Captain Juan Quadra who discovered Nootka Sound; he was there a year before Vancouver even saw the place. Sorry, explorers are not settlers. The savvy English—they do have a way of hogging the loot. Hostilities between Spain and England over British Columbia came to nothing. We read about Vancouver and admire that intrepid explorer but no one would envy his fate. Dead by the age of forty, he seems to have been a decent sort and deserved a better end. Well what can I say? After all other might-be aspirants, my pursuit leads to the erstwhile John Morton.

In the beginning things didn't go so well with John. Prospecting for gold was a waste and his business venture at brick making failed. Nonetheless he persevered and gave us a tale worth the read. My story is enriched by his adventures and although I shall heap praise upon his head, could he speak, he would surely say, "Who me? There must be some mistake. After all, while I was there for the first seven years, I later moved away, first to California and then to my farm in Mission." Yet for all the wanderings, those first seven years are enough for me. Thus with pen in hand I take the liberty to underscore the fact, despite any other distant competitors like Gassy Jack, John Morton was Vancouver's first English settler. I hope my story will fascinate my cherished reader as much as it charms me.

Chapter One
Canada: A Forbidding Place

When Jacques Cartier and the King of France met, it was a collaboration of two entrepreneurs who struck an agreement to search for "certain isles and countries where it is said there must be great quantities of gold and other riches." Cartier's voyage across the Atlantic led him to Labrador. He was not impressed and wrote in his journal,

"The land should not be called New Land being composed of stones and horrible rugged rocks….I did not see one cartload of earth and yet I landed in many places….there is nothing but moss and short, stunted shrub. I am rather inclined to believe this is the land God gave to Cain."

Beware of first impressions. Cartier's opinion of Canada improved as he sailed further west in the summer of 1534. His bigger problem as of yet lay undetected. In 1497, John Cabot had laid claim to Newfoundland for England. Furthermore, England and France were in perpetual conflict with unalterable circumstances that favoured England. On the surface, it might have looked like the other way round but France had a problem. The French were always preoccupied with other enemies right at their back door.

England had two advantages. The first was twenty-seven miles of salt water between Europe and their island kingdom that we call the English Channel. The other advantage was a larger Navy. The

Franco/English rivalry would play out in North America with a similar advantage for the English in North America. Instead of the Channel the Appalachian Mountains separated the French and the English. For the French these mountains were an adequate defense for a century but mountains can be easily crossed. Then came the American Revolution and the intrusion of the Empire Loyalists who flooded into British controlled Canada. That the British had conquered Quebec in 1759 was bad enough. The influx of Protestant immigrants had now made for controversy that would dominate Politics for the next two hundred years.

This is as good a time to raise the questions for reasons that would make anybody immigrate to a foreign land. Ask the Puritans why they settled in New England and they would have answered to establish a truly Christian country—ideally a New Jerusalem. Ask others and you might get something quite different. A more sophisticated and worldly answer might be the spirit of enterprise. Others might retort that it was for adventure. A more reasonable answer might be greed. The more practical answer might be the effort to escape poverty or perhaps a combination of all four. Whatever moved a generation to leave family and friends behind and strike out for the New World is testimony to a people who were ready to pay the high price of hardship, loneliness and fear. For some it proved to be a price too high and so—they returned to their homeland disillusioned and grateful promising themselves they would never do anything so foolhardy again.

In the 17th century the allure was fish. In the 18th century, it was furs. In the 19th century, it was gold. To their everlasting credit, the French got here first. Unfortunately for them In 1759, Montcalm lost the battle of the plains of Abraham. The French passed under the rule of England, which onerous as that might seem, was better than that of the Americans. Discontent is universal.

Intermarriage with First nations produced the Metis who were found not only in the Prairies, but as far west as British Columbia.

On the other hand the Americans suffering from a surplus of land hardly needed the frozen northlands and were content to let the 49th parallel separate them from the immigrants to the north. British Columbia was the exception especially when gold was discovered in the Cariboo. However, even that was not quite enough to risk a war with England especially when they were on the verge of a civil war amongst themselves. The only wrinkle in this arrangement was Vancouver Island that protruded below the 49th parallel. Britain managed to negotiate that issue even though they were six thousand miles away, which explains why they overlooked a minor detail with Point Roberts. Those wily Americans failed to mention that this ultimately invaluable piece of land also protruded below the 49th parallel and the English didn't notice. Perhaps it was for the best or Point Roberts would have looked like modern day Tsawwassen. Anyway, Point Roberts inhabited mostly by Canadians despite the 49th parallel, remains undeveloped and green—inconvenience of a border crossing notwithstanding.

In 1850 the major player in British Columbia was the Hudson's Bay Company and the last thing they wanted were settlers—yet the settlers came. The British Crown required oversight so they sent a representative to keep an eye on things. Richard Blanshard was the hapless choice. Dumped on Vancouver Island in 1849 where he wasn't wanted (the HBC would have said where he wasn't even needed) his salary was a lease of 1000 acres of undeveloped land. Alexander Begg writes,

> "Meanwhile, time hung heavily on Blanchard's hands. Set down upon the bare rocks of this mist enveloped isle, with a few of the only white people on it upon whom he was dependent for everything, for subjects, for society, and for creature comforts, who also were opposed to his rule in all their interests—he felt—utterly powerless and forlorn, and

could scarcely realize that he was governor, except by taking out his commission and reading it to himself occasionally."[4]

The next name on the list of notables is John Muir who came looking for coal and found it at Nainamo. Two years later he had shipped 2000 tons to San Francisco at twenty-eight dollars per ton. In the meantime, James Douglas had replaced Blanshard as governor at the munificent salary of 800 pounds Sterling per year because Victoria was showing a respectable population of 300. With a flourishing population of 80,000 first nations and a growing population of white settlers a judiciary was requited. Matthew B. Begbie, a bachelor would preside from 1859-1894. His was the privilege to keep order over a province that would boast a major shipping metropolis of 30,000 in the now renamed port that we know as Vancouver.

The world would hardly notice for a while because to them Canada and the frozen north had little to commend itself to the English immigrant who still preferred the more temperate climate of the United States. Immigrate to that uncultured wilderness called Canada? Only for the brave in heart, or for those whose stomachs were rolling from the blight of the European potato famine. Then came the news of the discovery of gold in British Columbia that flashed around world. Information that a newsmaker made possible by the incredible invention of the telegraph. (Think today's internet) Suddenly the great Fraser gold-rush of 1858 had primed the pump. Next came William Barker who struck it rich in the Cariboo, plus a few others in the pivotal year of 1858.

Enter Colonel Richard Clement Moody. His was the assignment to build a wagon road up the Fraser with the Royal Engineers. Next came the debate over the route. Victoria anticipating the dollar value of a deluge of prospectors argued for a route to the Cariboo by water

---

[4]   Alexander Begg, History of British Columbia, pp. 190, 191

(as far as that might be possible). Mainland entrepreneurs argued for a highway up the Fraser canyon as far away as Yale. Douglas saw the issues clearly. Open up the interior to the settlers to come, make the would-be prospectors pay for the road. The revenues were enormous. In the end Victoria prospered and so did the mainland.

One observer was not pleased. Having spent a decade in the British wild west, his description of Victoria in 1860 breathes the nostalgia of the irretrievable past.

> "I stand today upon the same spot, but oh! How changed. Of the twenty or thirty met before, but two or three answer to the call. Of the fields naught remains. The forest has been removed, and the bleak winds, unhindered now, rush into what was then a genial, sheltered place. The Beaver remains, but, great Jove! No more like the Beaver of former days than a coal barge is like a frigate. Mightier steamers float upon the harbour; the natives, once half a thousand, have disappeared; homes of the citizens occupy the fields; telegraph and telephone wires make the streets hideous; there is great hurry and scurry, but I doubt whether there is more happiness and content now than was enjoyed by the few but hospitable and kind-hearted Hudson Bay Company's residents in 1850."[5]

The nostalgia of the aforesaid raises the eternal questions especially when it comes to values and quality of life. Perhaps if we could raise our plaintive from the dead to let him see the Victoria of today he might change his mind. Unbeknown to the average Englishman, for a hundred years a few savvy entrepreneurs had been getting rich

---

5   Alexander Begg, The History of British Columbia, 219

from the fur trade. The native Indian population may have been dazzled by iron pots and the luxury of being able to boil water but Europeans had also been amazed at the speed of a birch-bark canoe. Toss in the pemmican of dried Buffalo meat and navigable rivers and suddenly you have travel at speeds which were hitherto considered impossible. In snowy winter the Northern European is virtually housebound. Imagine their surprise when they witnessed the native Indians defy drifted snow on snow shoes that made travel possible in winter. Long distances and snow, hitherto an impossible barrier, had been conquered by human ingenuity. For the first time the inexhaustible supply of Canadian furs was accessible to man. Now the pelts of northern Beaver were showing up in Europe where the demand was insatiable. The fur trade opened the doors for unimaginable adventure for many and unlimited wealth for the few.

Of course the price of progress depends upon your point of view.

The average British yeoman had no care for all of this, but when gold was discovered in British Columbia, that is a different matter. Furthermore the coming of ironclad ships and steam had made crossing the Atlantic something of an adventure within reach. At long last the appeal of an untouched country like Canada was beginning to capture the hearts of men with a yearning for adventure. The needed catalyst was gold. The decade of 1860-1870 would change the wintery country of Canada into an undreamed paradise. Into this decade a young Yorkshireman had come of age who lived in Saledine Nook, Yorkshire and his name was John Morton.

Chapter Two
The Three Greenhorns

Take a trip to Vancouver in 2018. Visit Harbour Centre and see the City from the Harbour House Revolving restaurant. Look down if you dare and scan Vancouver's golden mile. To the north is the Burrard Inlet. To the south is False Creek and Granville Island. Now look left to Stanley Park. Look down to Burrard Street, or in other words, Vancouver's fabled West End. Imagine how rich you would be if you owned all this land. Brace yourself.... one hundred and fifty-six years ago, three Yorkshire pioneers actually did. New Westminster in 1862 laughed at Samuel Brighouse, William Hailstone and John Morton, who pre-empted those 555 acres. One hundred and fifty years ago people called them the "three greenhorns." With the benefit of hindsight, were they alive today they would be singing a different tune. While Brighouse had image, it was John Morton who was the brains behind this fabled trio and with the help of his friends and a few natives built the very first house where now the Guinness Tower Building stands near the Marine Building.

Vancouver now had a landmark and a name. It was called "Morton's Shack." The splendour of that shack built of rough sawn boards attracted a motley audience of Indians with their woven blankets, and although Vancouver has enjoyed a facelift since those pioneer days, it has been a tourist attraction ever since.

William Hailstone, Samuel Brighouse, John Morton

One cannot go very far in this narrative without raising the question, where and what is home? Raise this topic with just about any Vancouverite you know and do it over lunch. The answer to our question could take multiple roads to just about any place on planet Earth. Anyone can leave home. Home doesn't move when one strikes out for a new location but the home where one grows up remains in the memories of the heart and cannot be erased. I have raised this question often enough to discover a lot of homesick people who will never return to the place of their birth and who also will never feel at home where they live because they are away from the source of their memories for ten, twenty, forty years or maybe even a lifetime.

For all the good fortune that befell the greenhorns, only one felt at home in the city of his choice. Fate took Hailstone and Brighouse back to England to be buried in what they knew was home, because both of them never felt that Vancouver was their home. Although Morton returned to England for lengthy visits, he lived his lifetime in and around the Vancouver area. When Morton saw the place in its original and untouched state, he had a vision of the city to come and loved its setting. He was awed by the vision's pristine beauty and the grandeur of the mountain setting. His love of the place was instant when he saw it, and that appreciation never left him. Vancouver was always John Morton's home right from the start and in his mind saw it as the "New Liverpool" of North America. Whoever wrote his obituary in the Vancouver Daily World, April 19, 1912 thought the same thing and wrote accordingly[6]. His gravesite, an obelisk, is in New Westminster's oldest cemetery—it can be visited by anyone. I have stood before that memorial stone and pondered this man and his life. He loved and lost his first wife who died giving birth to their second child. Morton not only knew hardship, he also knew tragedy—yet he lived to love again.

*The obelisk that marks the grave of John and Ruth Morton.
New Westminster Cemetery.*

---

6   The Vancouver Daily World wrote of John Morton, "Probably to a greater extent than any other resident of the Canadian west, he lived to enjoy the fruits of his days of pioneer labor and to see his early prophecies fully justified."

It is interesting to note than Jane Ann is recognized, although she was buried in Sapperton. Morton's second wife Ruth showed her generosity of spirit by inscribing the evidence in her recognition of John's first wife and mother of the two children she bore.

Pioneer life in British Columbia was severe to those who braved the perils of carving a new world out of the wilderness. Providence smiled on John Morton when he married his second wife, Ruth Mount, who now became the enduring love of his life. Before Morton died he gave the funds for the building of a church that was named after his beloved Ruth. It is called The Ruth Morton Memorial Baptist Church. It was the first of many tributes to be given to this intrepid woman. Its magnificent memorial stained glass window is a national treasure and a love tribute that, in my mind, makes the John and Ruth Morton story the best romance epic to come out of the Canadian West. Who needs the Taj Mahal? We've got our own right here in Vancouver where that lovely edifice (now renamed the Mountainview Community Church) still stands on the corner of Prince Albert Street and East 27th.[7] Not only is the story beautiful, so is the church. After this kind of landmark the remembrances diminish: A street (a single block long) with Morton's name that overlooks English Bay, a restaurant by the name of The Three Greenhorns (now out of business), a sundial that pays tribute to Morton and his friends, and after that, the archives of Vancouver's library plus our memories.

---

[7] The Ruth Morton Memorial Baptist Church was renamed when it amalgamated with Metropolitan Community Church in 2015. The beautiful memorial stained glass window that commemorates John and Ruth Morton remains.

Corner of Morton and Beach Ave, across the street is the sundial

The Sundial

The Beach Street Sundial was in honour of the three greenhorns. The inscription reads, "I mark my hours by shadow, mayest thou mark thine by sunshine." In my opinion the inscription best suits John Morton. He was the motivator of the three greenhorns. He was the indefatigable optimist who despite early failure and ill-conceived decisions never lost hope thus earning for himself the title of "first settler."

The amazing life of John Morton reads like a blockbuster movie. For melodrama and adventure, his story is unique. The loveable Morton missed some great opportunities that would have made him a multi-millionaire. Nonetheless, this indefatigable plodder and hardworking man one century ago amassed a fortune of $700,000 at a time when a labouring man was fortunate to be marking 22 cents an hour. Not bad for a novice who was eyewitness to some of the most exciting events you can imagine. That's why he's such a fascinating character a hundred and five years later, after he died. To trace the story detective like, we must make our way to rural England and to Yorkshire.

Chapter Three
Childhood

All the early Mortons were Scottish Presbyterians who moved to a village near Huddersfield. Soon after the accession of Queen Elizabeth to the throne of England in 1558, they opened a small chapel on their own property. No record has been preserved of the church, but it seems to have existed for many years. Next came the Puritans, which split the Anglican Church. Britain's civil quarrel with Charles the First brought Oliver Cromwell's independents and the roundheads. The ensuing war saw the defeat of Charles, and Cromwell's joyful army claimed the victory. One can only imagine the sound of 30,000 men singing hymns as they went into battle against the Royalist forces. Royal Roads Military Academy take note. (Alas, that became a civilian college in 1995.) Getting back to British history, the spinoff of Cromwell's era over time created the Baptist church as the independents looked for spiritual release after the coronation of Charles II.

The Morton clan is an example. These Bible reading folks did not adhere to their Presbyterian roots and the family meeting house had disappeared by 1739 when the first Baptist chapel was built there, the same year that John Wesley and his hymn-writing brother Charles burst upon the English scene. While acknowledging the Westminster Confession and their Psalm singing heritage, Baptists loved to sing those racy new hymns that were scandalizing the old folks. Isaac Watts had already made his mark with hymns like "O God Our Help in Ages Past," his Christmas carol, "Joy to the World," and my favourite hymn, "Join All the Glorious Names." Contemporary Rockers take note.

The Mortons loved to sing these hymns and John Morton was no exception. Today's TV generation goes to concerts. In Morton's day the congregation was the concert and everybody participated; so compared to the yesteryears, just who really had more fun? Was it the participants of older times or today's spectator audience? Getting back to the Mortons, many members of the family had been gathered into the Baptist Church soon after its formation. The birth of that church initiated a course of events that moulded the character of the Morton family with undertones that ultimately reached into the new world.

In 1713, exactly two hundred years before the Vancouver Ruth Morton Memorial Church was dedicated, a letter registered in the name of Michael Morton was being written to the queen. Its contents reveal a request for permission to build a meeting house as provided for under the *Toleration Act for Protestant Dissenters Worship*. Although permission was received, the project languished for lack of funds for twenty-five years until at last a wealthier member of the Morton family by the name of Joseph provided the land and the funds. The church was no longer an unfulfilled dream and was dedicated in 1739. The style of the architecture was Greek. Standing in mute contrast to English Gothic, it reflected the spirit of English nonconformity that revelled in the newest thing. The Mortons seemed to have filled the position of chapel stewards, rendering to the community outstanding services, but always in that quiet non-ostentatious manner which seems to have become one of the traditions of this church.

Salendine Nook Baptist Church, Yorkshire, England

Into this intensely religious heritage John Morton was born on April 6, 1834, the first of four sons, along with six sisters. Every indication points to a frugal background suggesting that his father Joseph was struggling even though his pottery business flourished into a prosperous enterprise which would bypass John in favour of his younger brothers. John was "a frank young fellow with a smile in his eyes" but little is known of his early life, except that he was the proverbial optimist who loved to sing hymns, especially when the youth of his Baptist church met on Monday evening. His knowledge of bricklaying reveals that he understood the kilns of a pottery. His social needs were met through the young people who attended the Salendine Nook Baptist Chapel. (Leave it to the British to come up with those charming names for a village — Salendine Nook!)

The building where John Morton was born

For congregational singing, the Sunday evening service was primetime entertainment. The modern nineteenth century invention of gaslights had transformed village life. Now churches could be illumined after dark, making the auditorium as "bright as day." For the first time after dark, the young people had a choice between the family fireplace or the church. In many ways the social dynamic of the village pub was not dissimilar to the church. Share your joys and burdens, it makes you feel so much better—in the case of the pub there was the temptation to squander your joy money for beer, in the case of the church you could be intoxicated with just the joyous singing. This author has at times longed for a time machine that could have taken him back 200 years to Salendine Nook and join John Morton singing Charles Wesley's "O For a Thousand Tongues to Sing my Great Redeemer's Praise." (The English tune is so much better than the common "Frazer" tune we sing in North America.) John Morton was present to witness the building of the first addition to the church he loved so dearly. It had to be enlarged to accommodate the crowds who thronged the church after dark because it could now be illumined with light. Imagine eight hundred people on a Sunday evening with a victory march around the church aisles to celebrate the new converts. Such was the magnetic attraction of congregational singing. Furthermore there was no competition; theatres, radio and television had yet to come. (Today's generation is oblivious to the fact that the phenomenon of congregational singing at the evening service would spread throughout the English-speaking world. The closest rival to this experience is the local high school football game, but the only skill required here is the ability to scream enthusiastically. Through the week, families like the Mortons would gather around the piano and the spinoff was an old-fashioned song fest and it didn't matter if Uncle Harry sang too loud when he was off key. Banter and laughter accompanied these events especially when once a year the Christmas Carols were sung.

I was fortunate enough to be alive when this phenomenon was still current. By 1949, the Sunday evening service was ailing, but at Central Baptist Church in London, Ontario we could still count on 700 showing up for the evening service and the balcony was packed with young people. The singing of a congregation or a crowd is a unique and very satisfying expression of the soul that many contemporary Canadians have never experienced. The Sunday evening church service in that last twentieth century singing decade has been eclipsed by television and I'm not so sure we are better off. Today's generation knows a lot about grooving with the music but my generation remembers with regretful nostalgia the day when *we were the music*. Have I made my point? John Morton loved to sing and so do I, provided there are others to drown out my mistakes when I'm singing a little off key.

Two hundred years later the Salendine Nook Baptist church is still standing and has an active congregation. Its natural lines of Greek architecture give it a beauty and simplicity that suited the character of its worshippers. Morton loved his church and in appreciation held its benefactors in esteem. Acquainted with both his heritage and the Joseph of 1739 (likely his great-great-grandfather) the young John Morton never forgot his debt of gratitude to the memory of these men and ultimately transplanted this legacy with similar deeds here in British Columbia.

Morton had the privilege of being alive in the fabulous sixties (1860-1890's that is). What a time for that privileged young man to enjoy. Thanks to the repeal of the Corn Laws, which favoured the rich (no wonder the wealthy successfully opposed it for so long) the common people were eating better. Still John Morton could not understand his discontent. Morton the restless had not succumbed to the appeal of the British army that would have him fight the Crimean war. One of the reasons why he was alive to be amazed at the information age introduced to the world by the telegraph. That's how he learned about the gold rush in British Columbia. Thousands of miles away like most Englishmen, he could read of a heroine like Florence Nightingale who would advocate for the education of women and even suggest rights to vote before the average Englishman had been given the franchise. Choosing adventure for security, his would be the privilege to meet and know Gassy Jack and his tavern known by every Vancouverite that ever lived in Vancouver's pioneer days. Given his Christian family heritage, he probably saved his pennies because, Morton was an abstainer. Being something of an historian, he admitted that when Gassy Jack opened his saloon, "things began to liven up a bit." So now we have to answer the question, how did John Morton ever make it to a land so remote from his comfortable pew in Yorkshire, England.

Like so many who come from a church background, John at times was restless and curious about the world beyond the shores of Britain. While Morton knew that the Canadian frontier had very few churches, he esteemed his Christian values practicing his faith by deeds; for example, he kind to first nation people. Morton would be separated from family life for over a decade. He would eventually return to his Baptist roots but not until later years. With the Morton foundry to inherit, one has to ask the question why would the eldest son leave home and pass the business to his younger siblings. Could it be that John was a little rebellious? Did this would-be-adventurer have conflicts with his father Joseph? Why would the potential owner of the family business cast his eye on the new world for is future? It is not too difficult to imagine his peers shaking their heads at such a reckless voyageur.

To his mother's chagrin, he avoided girls and the prospects of an early marriage, which would have tied him to Yorkshire. Instead, came a mother's worst fears; Morton would strike out on his own to the new world. With all the promises of a young man's assurances to return, Joseph and his wife Rhoda like so many others would surely wonder, "Will we ever see our son again?" They were to be rewarded for that painful separation. John did return, and like Sinbad the sailor regale them with his new world stories of achievement. Mercifully, they lived to rejoice in the ventures of their enterprising son.

Brickworks where John Morton learned his trade

Chapter Four
The New World

The names Spuzzum and Craigellachie would mean nothing to the ordinary Englishman and Morton was no exception. Explained later in the annals of history, their meaning would intimidate many. Morton would eventually learn what they meant. Interpreted, they should have represented terror and regret. Morton would shrug his shoulders and soldier on until he proved himself the worthy man he became. For the present, Morton would not be able to explain his discontent, that is, until his awakening.

When John Morton was twenty-four, gold was discovered on the Fraser River in far-off British Columbia. Subsequently, gold would be discovered at the mouth of the Quesnel, at Quesnel Forks, Keithley Creek, Antler Creek and then at Williams Creek. Cornwall sailor Billy Barker made $1,000 in two days (eventually he made $600,000). He was the exception that proved the rule. Many followed his example! A few reaped a similar reward. Overnight the Bank of British Columbia was open for business in London. The Cariboo gold rush was on, and by the spring of 1861 it had become a stampede. News of the gold strikes spread world-wide and glowing accounts of easily made fortunes found their way into the news sheets of Huddersfield, of which Salendine Nook was a suburb. By some means John Morton learned about the rush and convinced himself that he had as good a chance at the gold as anyone. Persuading his cousin Sam Brighouse to join him, Morton announced their decision to venture on what must have seemed to many like a fool's errand. Their minds made up, the young men staked their meagre savings on one-way tickets that would ultimately bring them to British Columbia. They gambled on striking it rich enough to return. And return they did, but their fortunes were not made in gold.

The Great Eastern Steamship

On May 8, 1862, the steamship Great Eastern (that laid the first trans-Atlantic cable) began her fourth trans-Atlantic voyage from Milford Haven, Britain (Wales) to New York with an obscure John Morton aboard. In contrast to Morton, Isambard Kingdom Brunel was the most famous shipbuilder alive and he had a dream. He would build the greatest ship ever constructed with a double steel hull. Why not? He was a shipbuilding tycoon with a world reputation. Like the still-to-come Titanic it was to be the greatest ship afloat. Like the Titanic it was destined to become a boondoggle. In contrast to one of his first customers, John Morton, (who was eventually to build a fortune the slow hard way), the tycoon was destined to blow himself out. His financial venture would be a money loser from day one and may have precipitated his early death at age fifty-three. His ultimate disgrace came when the ship that cost a half a million pounds was sold for a trifling twenty-five thousand for scrap. This was a sorrow that Brunel would not live to witness. In other words he went from riches to rags—the opposite kind of story from that of Brunel's undistinguished passenger John Morton.

The Great Eastern was 692 feet long with a beam of 82 feet, weighed 18,915 tons, and was the marvel of that age. For a ship that had garnered a reputation all out of proportion to its worth, and although it would become a classic failure in the annals of seagoing vessels, she was a marvel to behold. With her six masts and four smokestacks and massive paddlewheels, she must have been an awesome sight for John Morton and Sam Brighouse as they went aboard. On the ship they met William Hailstone. The trio of Yorkshire men became fast friends and entered into a shipboard pact that bound them to share resources and fortunes as fate would decide. Little did they dream of the amazing future that awaited them. Three men who couldn't have been unlikelier characters had forged their mutual destiny: Morton, the optimist, Brighouse the pragmatist and Hailstone, the grouch. The shipboard pact joined Brighouse and Hailstone with the ingenuity and foresight of John Morton, a combination that paid a handsome dividend.

These novice adventurers had read of the civil war that was raging in America but that war had seemed so far away. Now they were about to taste the inconvenience. Fortunately they were only travelling through America to get to British Columbia. Had they been immigrants they might have experienced what so many young Europeans discovered: come to America and be straightway drafted into the army. With no motivation whatever except to escape the poverty of Europe many male immigrants found themselves with a rifle in their hands facing the slaughterhouse of the American Civil War.

New York in 1862

When the greatest ship afloat docked at New York, Morton, Brighouse and Hailstone cast curious eyes on the new world. One wonders what they might have thought to see this bustling seaport with its 3,000 horse drawn wagons in crowded alleys complete with their smells and effluent. Arriving in New York at the time the Civil War was raging certainly made life challenging for our newly arrived Englishmen. The Daily Tribune was full of this tragic story, which at this time was going badly for the North. Some Englishmen were even predicting the South would win which would solve the problem of English Mills that were running out of cotton. Abraham Lincoln's blockade of the Southern Ports was effective and the Union Navy had proven their worth. Gradually things turned in favour of the North and we know how that story turned out. The Civil War compelled our three adventurers to take the circuitous route by way of St. Louis.

Reflecting the British mindset at the time, their sympathies would have been with the North. That they could, as outsiders, begin their journey in the North and finish at the port of Houston in the South is a curious anomaly. Wouldn't that be interesting material for an interview? Recalling the story, Morton's son Joseph, years after related, "The three traveled together to New York and from there by way of St.

Louis and the Union Pacific Railway, then under construction, down to the gulf of Mexico with a frigate to Panama." For those who might like to ask the question, what did these travelers think about slavery? Young Joseph further recounted, "Father told me that whilst traveling on the Union Pacific, it was necessary upon one occasion to stop the train for a quarter of an hour to let the buffalo pass or rather—to work through them. The buffalo were crossing the track and were strung out as far as he could see in all directions." On another occasion the Yorkshire trio detrained for a stretch to walk. It was then they saw a dead man lying in a ditch and stopped to investigate. A stranger noticing Morton and his friends sneered, "Don't bother, it's only a nigger." These Englishmen ignoring what they saw wisely postponed discussion because they had a destination that would remove them from such prejudice for the time being. They would face racial issues again when they confronted the First Nations of Canada. One can only speculate on how they felt about racial issues. More on this subject in the next chapter.

Another prospector from Yorkshire had arrived five years earlier. His name was William Duncan, however with this difference, Duncan came in search of heavenly gold. A missionary sponsored by the Anglican Church Missionary Union, he was prospecting for souls. Eventually he won thousands to Christianity and built a church to seat 1200. His vision prompted the setting up of a separate Indian community—the utopian Metlakatla. Like the Puritans of the Massachusetts Colony, it was to be a city set on a hill but the occupants were to be first nations' people. For fifteen years, it seemed to have succeeded. This Christian community prospered and brought education and enlightenment. Sadly, twenty years later, the white man's diseases had done its work. Many of the newly converted Indians were dead. The tragedy that befell the First Nations was not foreseen, nor could it have been avoided. They had not been exposed to diseases that Europeans took for granted; therefore they had not built up the necessary immunities. Morton would have approved of William Duncan: Brighouse and Hailstone would have been indifferent.

Returning to our story and the three Yorkshire travelers, we find them in transit, spectators to the conflagration of the American Civil war but not participants. Grist for many conversations no doubt, as the News of that titanic struggle would dominate the Newspapers of even faraway Victoria.

Buffalo were often killed just for sport

The travels of Morton and his two companions demonstrate the folly of the American Civil War. To get to Texas from St. Louis required a train trip through rebel territory, yet the ticket was purchased in Union territory. These travelers had no difficulty since they were merely Englishmen using the railroads to get to their destination. Texas exemplifies the ambivalence of the Southwest American pioneers who were against the north but pragmatic enough to know that "business is business."

In his Vancouver book, Allan Morley relates, "Catching a ship for Panama, they crossed the isthmus probably on the Panama Trans-Isthmian Railroad which had been completed seven years earlier.

Without delay they boarded a vessel bound for San Francisco and from there to Victoria."

Arriving at their destination, once again the Negro question faced John Morton. When he got to Victoria he spotted a "nigger" paying for his licence to prospect for gold and drew the appropriate conclusion. As for racism, Morton always treated the First Nations people with respect. Morton would not have made a good pioneer within the Confederate States of America.

The three gold seekers did not know that they were already too late. The Cariboo Gold Rush was now a year old and had already attracted droves of all types and conditions of men: miners and would-be miners, packers and storekeepers, gamblers and saloon-keepers. Yes, it even brought camels to the trail (they didn't last long) and hurdy-gurdy girls for the dance halls. It lured adventurers from the United States, from Britain, from Europe, and from Australia.

It brought the Overlanders (and what a story that is) from eastern Canada, who risked danger and even death on steep mountain trails that were foreign to their experience. All of this was as yet unknown to the Yorkshire men. Dangers still unknown have no power over the young. The folk who should really have been afraid were the First Nations. The influx of 30,000 newcomers carried a hidden array of diseases including smallpox for which native people had no immunities. In four years time 20,000 in British Columbia would die; about one third of the native population. For the Haida originals make that ninety percent of their tribe. European settlers had the advantage of centuries of immunizing exposure and while some still could die, most did not. The indigenous tribes of North America were in process of virtual extermination by starvation, war, and the invisible hand of disease.[8]

Unaware of the White Man's Menace and with high hopes and visions of virgin gold country the three disembarked at Victoria,

---

8   See Arthur J. Ray, I have Lived Here Since the World Began, p.191

(previously a quiet trading village of 300) a town of false-fronted wooden stores, shacks, hotels, and saloons, all flung together to meet the torrent of newcomers headed for the fields of gold. What a contrast this roaring, brawling, bustling town must have seemed in comparison to the neat brick homes of Salendine Nook. Here they registered with Governor James Douglas (destined to distinguish himself in Canadian history) and booked passage for New Westminster.

To give some idea of contrasting architecture and the emotions it can elicit, I cite from my personal experience. I shall never forget how charmed I was by the scenery and homes of Yorkshire the first time I saw it. I contrast this with another beautiful place called Provence in France. There is a striking difference in architecture and setting.

Historically, England as an island nation was a sheltered country without the fear of sudden invasions. In contrast to the warring tribes of Europe, its towns and villages are built by rivers and valleys. In Europe and especially in southern France, towns were built on hilltops that could be more easily defended from destructive armies. Windy in winter, they are so unlike an English town sequestered by a river and surrounded by tree top hills. Furthermore, the dominant architecture in southern France is masonry of stucco in contrast to England, where houses are mostly built of brick. This was especially true of Yorkshire where brick is king. Such is the reason for the quaint beautiful villages and towns of England. Americans from Michigan and New York State especially take note of the dramatic change they experience when they visit Ontario for the first time. New York and Michigan build their houses out of wood siding because brick is expensive and has to be shipped in from elsewhere. Like Yorkshire, Ontario is a place where brick is common and it affects the landscape. While American homes are larger, Ontario homes give the appearance of durability because brick wears long and is charming.

And speaking of Americans—the "greenhorns" were now getting acquainted with a few more. The influx of the Californian gold seekers had subsided to some extent but there were several thousand more who proudly related their tales of swagger and bravado. To the credit of the English negotiators and the authority of the British navy (a few British warships in the Pacific that the Americans couldn't match helps to settle important issues) the boundary dispute was settled with the 49th parallel as the line of demarcation in 1845. (The Americans wanted to dissect Vancouver Island with the southern part ceded to the USA.) Seems some gold-seeking Americans had forgotten all this and would have precipitated a war when somebody reminded them they were in Canada, not America.

Prior to Morton's arrival in 1858, some thousands of American prospectors thought a campaign to exterminate Indians would be a helpful idea. (Apparently, they were unaware that Governor Douglas was married to a Metis.) They were dissuaded of this by some very forceful action by Douglas who at the time pitted British authority against guns and won the day. But not until after the Fraser Valley war had petered out. History lovers take note, this all happened at Spuzzum, thirty-one miles north of Yale (50 kilometres). That little skirmish had cost about two hundred American lives, (depending on which version you believe). It had all begun with the rape of an Indian woman and an act of revenge that resulted in the decapitation of a pair of Frenchmen. Next event that happened was a few thousand Americans with rifles—mobilized to exterminate the Indians. They subscribed to the then current American wild west policy of "the only good Indian is a dead Indian." When in the night somebody discharged a rifle, the battle took place in the dark. The only problem was that there weren't any Indians around so they simply imagined their presence and started firing at anyone who moved. The following morning the dead Americans were counted. Who knows how many really died? The tally was reported to be a few dozen to a couple of thousand. Rumour spread the results and you believed what you will. The folly soon died out, with Governor Douglas taking charge, but not before an avalanche of accusers and victims were attempting to put one another in jail. Such was the fate of some American gold-seekers.

Even though four years had passed when our three English adventurers arrived, you can understand why Canadians were afraid that the USA might try to annex the Province especially if the Union armies of the North won the war. With this appreciation, one can imagine what was going through the minds of these Yorkshire men when they looked at ramshackle Victoria in 1862 thronging with men half of whom were from the country our trio had traversed to get to their destination. It is one thing to get three English adventurers into the new world, it is quite another to get England out of these pioneers. Only one really made the transition and that was John Morton. Meanwhile, Governor Douglas could put their minds at ease since this was 1862 and now the gun slinging Americans could speculate about one another in civil war while Douglas wrestled British Columbia into the newly created Canada in just another five years.

Chapter Five
It's an Indian World

On June 25, 1862, the sailing vessel Reliance, under Captain John Irving, departed from Esquimalt and made for Georgia Strait. She carried a cosmopolitan crowd: Scotsmen, Englishmen, Frenchmen, Dutchmen and Americans, all headed for the Cariboo. Quoting J.H. Grant, as Morton looked out at the mouth of the Fraser, "He gazed in wonder at the delta's waving forests of cattail from whence came the quacking, squawking, and gabbling of thousands of nesting geese and ducks. Gulls fluttered about, blackbirds sang in the rushes, cranes trumpeted, and bitterns boomed and gurgled." Later that afternoon they arrived at New Westminster. It would be sixteen years before Morton would again see the neat brick cottages of Salendine Nook.

New Westminster from the Fraser River, 1865

For all its shortcomings as a city, New Westminster in 1862 was nonetheless the gateway to the interior. At first, like that of other newcomers, John Morton's interest in the town was purely practical. He and his companions stopped and bought supplies before heading off for Yale and the Cariboo, but how does one resist the temptation to look around?

Morton and his friends, eager as they were to get to the golden fields, were also extremely curious to explore the sights and sounds of New Westminster. Strolling down Columbia Street, Morton passed a show window at a Merchant's store where he noticed a lump of coal prominently displayed. With knowledge of clay deposits learnt from childhood days in and around the pottery, Morton's mind ran to thoughts of kilns and bricks. Building materials in the pioneer setting were at a premium, and bricks were impossible to come by. In John Morton's heart, a business venture was conceived. The birth would come later and prove to be a bust.

Stepping into the store, Morton enquired about the origin of the sample. The merchant informed him that a native had brought in the coal the previous week and that the Indian had been in the store earlier that day. With a description of the man, Morton set out in hot pursuit on the trail that led northeast, in the direction of the Indian's home. The Englishman overtook his man half way to the east end of Burrard Inlet.

Because neither man could speak the language of the other, they engaged in a vigorous game of charades, in which Morton patiently imparted the tenor of his quest. The Indian, taking advantage of the opportunity to turn his superior knowledge into cash, agreed to show Morton the deposit of coal.

A few days later Morton and the Indian, carrying a heavy box of provisions and blankets, were on the twelve mile 1860 military trail from New Westminster to Burrard Inlet, heading for the coal seam. (Ever carry a too-heavy suitcase two blocks to catch a plane?) The Indian knew no English whatever, and Morton but one word of indigenous language: "Skookum." Quoting J.H. Grant who interviewed Morton, "'Skookum' he used on all occasions, often to the evident amusement of any native tribesman. When he understood his guide's gesture, the Englishman nodded his head and said, 'Skookum.' If he didn't he shook his head and said 'Skookum' to express his readiness in engaging click clack tonal conversation as they imparted to Morton's guide a message of absorbing significance, completely beyond the understanding of the Yorkshire man."

After encamping overnight, Morton and his guide took a dugout canoe to navigate Burrard Inlet. Morton would recall the beauty of that day. Sunshine and snow-capped mountains, blue water and untouched landscape filled his vision with wonder. A most jarring experience would soon leave an indelible mark on Morton's memory. At Brockton Point, two thousand natives were gathered for war. What must Morton have thought? What would anyone think about such a threatening and unfamiliar sight? They dare not ignore the war party. I suppose they were tempted to do otherwise but in reality no escape was possible. They beached the canoe and a lively debate ensued between Morton's guide and an Indian warrior – none of which Morton could understand or appreciate. Later he learned they were inviting the guide and Morton to join an anticipated tribal war, but the guide declined the invitation. Fortunately for all concerned, the battle never materialized. Meantime, the niceties of good manners had been observed and Morton was safe. He and his guide were free to continue their journey.

Now they could see smoke from the native huts dissolving into the azure sky; skins of animals, sides of fish and garish garments hung on trees and drying racks. From the canoe, Morton could see the children with their pet dogs enjoying the same kind of frolic as Morton remembered when he was a child. From time to time, men and women gathered on the shore to call their greetings to the explorers in the canoe.

The camp was only temporary. The Squamish bands had gathered there from various settlements to defend themselves against the expected raid from the Haidas to the north. The Haidas, in great black canoes measuring up to seventy feet long, were capable of sweeping down from the Queen Charlotte Islands onto the tribes of the south where they burned villages, killed the resisters, and carried off the remaining men, women, and children as slaves.

Time for a review. Put yourself in Morton's shoes. Newly introduced to these tribal tales, some true but most fanciful, what does one believe? He has just maneuvered a once-in-a-lifetime experience. What of his Indian guide? Can he trust him? Here is an Englishman who has never seen a native person except in a one-to-one encounter with others around. Can't you see the worried look on his face? There is no mistaking the intent of the Squamish, but still, Morton must have wondered. To make matters worse, one of the chieftains had just hailed Morton's guide and in no uncertain terms made some critical point. Furthermore Morton had just witnessed his guide objecting to a conscription effort for war. His native guide had just successfully resisted a persuasive oratory to join the warriors for battle. To Morton's relief, at last his indigenous guide had been given the clearance he pleaded for. Morton can breathe a little easier as they paddle their canoe away. But where is this stranger leading him as they paddle further and further away from the safety of other white men? (Had all this taken place in our generation with the wake of ocean going vessels they would have capsized). Rounding what is now Stanley Park, they made their way to the peaceful shores of English Bay.

Once again quoting Morley: "Morton gazed upon the white sands of English Bay sweeping upward before him. The guide beached his canoe while Morton, rapt with wonder, thought of Blackpool and of the panorama now before his eyes. While Morton stood appreciating the splendour of unspoiled English Bay, his newfound friend caught a few flounders for their lunch. That night the men slept under the trees. 'I was awakened in the morning,' Morton said, 'by a strange sound. I looked up and at first I thought a hundred pairs of trousers had just taken flight. I rubbed my sleepy eyes. A flock of cranes had evidently spent the night in the trees around us.' "

The guide cached his canoe and, beckoning to Morton, started into the forest in a north-westerly direction. At this point Morton had had enough and objected, fearful of being lost or something worse. His newfound friend persisted until at last Morton gave in. Somewhere near the present Denman Street, they came upon a footpath. It was an old trail leading from the canoe landing on False Creek directly across the peninsula and to Morton's surprise (and may I add delight) to the previous night's campsite on Coal Harbour. Suddenly the penny dropped and Morton perceived that Stanley Park, as we now know it, was almost an island connected by a link of land to what today we call the West End. Subsequently learning that the first narrows was sixty feet deep, Morton came to understand the significance of the natural geographic factors that would eventually create a metropolis we now call Vancouver. Fast forward 109 years.

On June 26, 1971 with a $500.00 grant from the City of Vancouver, our church (Ruth Morton Memorial Baptist) celebrated a re-enactment of the coming of John Morton to Burrard Inlet.[9] My son Mark played the part of the Indian guide and Henry Fietje, a church member, played the part of John Morton. CBC filmed the event and it was broadcast on British Columbia TV three times and once right across all of Canada.

Camping overnight at the foot of Main Street by the CN steamships dock, (where Morton and his guide camped in 1862), they then braved the perils of a very active shipping day. One steamer nearly capsized them. The two retraced the route of John Morton rounding Stanley Park and finishing up at Brockton Point on English Bay where deputy mayor, Art Phillips welcomed the reincarnated John Morton. In the afternoon, we had a parade down Fraser Street and in the evening a concert overlooking English Bay. On Sunday we did a re-enactment of Willard Litch and Morton taking a horse drawn buggy ride from the West End over the Cambie bridge finishing off at the church building that was still only a vision in 1912 by Morton and Litch.

---

9   In 1971, I was the pastor of the Ruth Morton Memorial Baptist Church. In collaboration with CBC and a grant of $500 from the City of Vancouver, we did a re-enactment of the coming of John Morton to Burrard Inlet.

*My Son Mark played the part of the Indian Guide.
Henry Fietje played the part of John Morton.*

Our re-enactment begins Saturday June 26, 1971

The Float: On display in the parade Saturday afternoon.

Vancouver was destined to become a world-renowned harbour. Morton had just come to Burrard Inlet via the Panama Railroad. He instinctively knew that east west trade would require a harbour like this. In 1862 the world was abuzz about the Suez Canal that was under construction. Did those thoughts enter Morton's mind? Perhaps but to be sure if Morton's vision of a world class harbour had the addition of expertise, that knowledge alone could have made him a millionaire if he had been able to exploit it. As it was, Morton's judgement *shaped by his old country experiences and learning,* was not able to comprehend the wealth potential that lay untouched all about him. Morton would ultimately prosper, but not until others had made a fortune out of the resources that lay at his feet. Morton relayed this epochal day again and again to his wife Ruth. In later years she would say, "John was struck by the beauty of the harbour and knew there and then that he had found the place where he wanted to spend a lifetime." He even had a name for it—New Liverpool.

Meanwhile, Morton returned to New Westminster and shared his experiences with his partners, who were now anxious to be off to the goldfields. They might better have spared their efforts; they were already by the pot of gold at the end of the rainbow but were oblivious to the nature of its disguised wealth. For example, take the 135 feet tall forest timbers that dominated their land. The greenhorns were oblivious to the standing wealth of the forest timber that abounded everywhere one looked.

Chapter Six
Faded Gold

The summer had scarcely begun and the weather was good for travel. Supplies had to be chosen carefully. Morton even counted horseshoe nails; not too many, one mustn't risk too much; twenty-two, to be exact (leftovers from a friend who gave them to John). With a whimsical smile he explained to his friends that horseshoe nails might well be in short supply in the Cariboo, and worth a small fortune to some horse owner in need of them. Eventually, after packing the nails, Morton, Brighouse and Hailstone set out in a paddle wheeler, likely for Yale, the jumping off spot for the many mining camps which had sprung up like mushrooms along the road to Cariboo. The "greenhorns" might have taken the Cariboo Wagon Road up the Fraser Valley. Some of it had been built by the time they got there. At other times, like so many others, they may have trekked their way north on the "River Trail" far below.

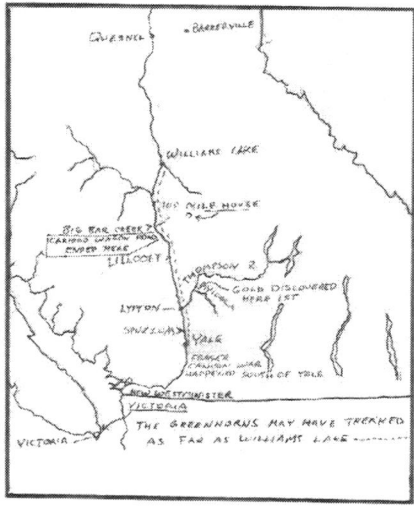

Map of the Cariboo Wagon Road

The challenge of the goldfields was heightened by stories of easy wealth. Prospectors had astonishing tales of pebbles of gold so easily scooped up by the handfuls—wealth for the asking. Those lucky exceptions belied the truth. Experience proved otherwise and the task— daunting, to say the least. Pick up a modern-day map of British Columbia with its highways and far flung communities which even by contemporary standards are remote. Imagine yourself in Yale with your backpack, groceries and equipment, making plans to hike to Lillooet. To boot, you are in a race with others to get there first. Sound appealing? Most of us would say, "Forget it!" Many did, but Morton and his friends mastered the challenge without reward. How does one feel having trekked 800 miles with nothing to show for it?

Most sources have the Yorkshire trio making the journey to the goldfields via the Fraser and Yale. Morton's son Joseph suggests this. Perhaps they took this route on their second trip to the Cariboo in 1863, as most likely they journeyed the Lillooet River route on the first since the Fraser trail wasn't opened until 1863. Either way, the difficult trail from Yale stretched northward 235 miles, and over it thousands of men had "trudged their way on their feet which became blistered with warts. Backs ached. Eyes became gritty from the wind-blown particles of sand. In the canyons one foot placed carelessly on that rocky ledge and all the road there was, might have sent a weary traveler hurtling down to the roaring, boulder-strewn waters of the river, hundreds of feet below."

The Yorkshire men had plenty of company on the journey. Miners, trappers, traders—men of every kind—struggling and sweating with their packs on their backs over the long trail, all of them eager to reach Eldorado, to stake claims before others could get in ahead of them. At their destination the three discovered that some had already become wealthy with astonishing rapidity. But like most others, they themselves were not so lucky. John Morton had made a wise decision to bring the horseshoe nails; he sold them for a dollar each.

Those were lawless days but the story of British law and order was infinitely better than that of the '49ers in California. The following incident related by Joseph Morton is revealing: "Father told me that while they were on their way in on one of their trips, I do not know which one, he took a little pail to get some fresh water for supper from the lake, and just as he was dipping the pail into the water, noticed a corpse in the water. After examining it, he moved off to one side to another place to get some clean water. He got his water, took it back to their bivouac, told his two companions of what he had seen, and they all returned to the corpse to view it. It was then noticed that the head had been smashed in, so they looked around for further evidence, finding two more bodies, three in all—all with their heads smashed in." One can imagine thoughts of the trio with such a tragic discovery. When the weather turned bad in the fall, the dispirited and discouraged men decided to clear out before it got worse.

On more than one morning in those early winter days the men awoke to a fresh snowfall of three to six inches. Joseph comments, "Father also remarked to me on how they slept in the snow, and how, in the morning, the first one up would see two mounds of snow on the ground, 'like a graveyard,' to use Father's own words."

How long the return trip to New Westminster must have seemed to the dispirited men, one can only imagine. The hardships of the trail were difficult enough. Without the incentive of gold fever one wonders what was going through their minds. Returning, the weary travelers had no prospects of quickly earned wealth and a long winter lay ahead. As the trio trudged their way back to New Westminster, Morton's thoughts returned to his summer experience with the Indians. Perhaps he had been too hasty in his evaluation of the coal seam. Might there not be clay of better quality if one took a little more time to look? Visions of an infant industry producing bricks once again crossed his mind.

When the three men returned to New Westminster they had traveled no less than 800 miles, more than 470 of it on foot. They had not discovered gold but they were on the verge of something better. The three men returned to the site of Coal Harbour to investigate.

Chapter Seven
The Best of Possible Worlds

On the morning of October 3rd, 1862, the trio set out for the coal seam, this time with Morton as guide. Retracing his steps, Morton led his companions to Coal Harbour. Climbing the bluff, they discovered top grade clay suitable for bricks. The vision of an infant pottery industry boggled their minds. Morton's business venture was reborn.

Morton set out for the land office where Chartres Brew, the Justice of the Peace, presided. J.H.Grant notes, "Brew had come out from England to assist Judge Matthew Baillie-Begbie, but as Begbie was quite capable of dispensing all the justice necessary, Brew spent much of the time on other matters. An enthusiastic westerner, he made a careful study of everything pertaining to the coast, and encouraged men to take up land and become permanent settlers." Brew explained to Morton the niceties of the law, and in compliance with the newly-born highest tribunals of the times, the Yorkshire men were about to make the decision of a lifetime.

Imagine—they are going to buy land that nobody else wants. How? Easy, decide what you desire and walk around it. Payment is in services rendered as needed by the government. It would take about seven years. From time to time when government needed labour, you did your turn. Morton and his partners measured their own land, driving their first stake into what is now the 1900 Block of West

Georgia, where the old horseshow building stood for half a century. Now having walked around about 555 acres, it was time for action. On November 3rd Morton filed, in the names of all three men, what later became District Lot 185, which spans from Burrard Street to Stanley Park, and from Burrard Inlet to English Bay.

The historic document reads as follows:

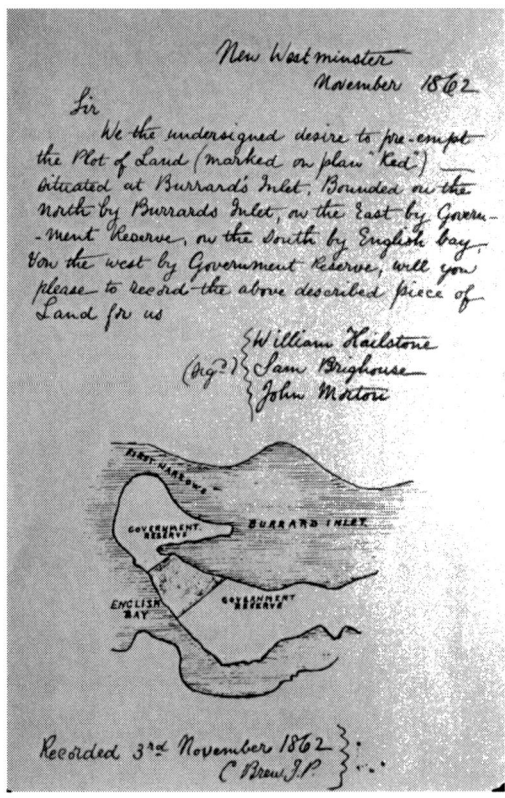

New Westminster

November 1862

Sir

We the undersigned desire to pre-empt the Plot of Land (marked on plan "Red") — situated on Burrard's Inlet, Bounded on the North by Burrards Inlet, on the East by Government Reserve, on the South by English Bay, & on the west by Government Reserve, will you please to record the above described piece of Land for us

Signed {William Hailstone
Sam Brighouse
John Morton

Recorded 3rd November 1862, C Brew J.P.

When making the first survey of today's West End, the Royal Engineers wrote across the plan: Brickmaker's Claim. They additionally noted: "Heavy Timbered Land, very swampy in places."

The pre-emption cost was a total of $555.75. As I have explained cash was not really required. Pre-emptions were commonly paid for by working out the sum on the roads or other local improvements carried out by the government. Never in the annals of Canadian history was so much valuable land acquired for so little. Like the Dutch who purchased Manhattan for $22, our trio made the deal of a lifetime. Years ago, when my high school professor wanted to make a point he speculated that a penny invested 2,000 years ago at three percent interest compounded semi-annually would today be worth over ten million dollars, if you could live so long to collect it. Morton and his friends would not have to live so long. In their own lifetime, they saw their investment pay off handsomely.

New Westminster was not impressed by their acquisition. The townsfolk laughed at their naiveté and dubbed them the "Three English Greenhorns." In view of the unoccupied countryside that abounded immediately adjacent to New Westminster, the investment seemed like a poor choice; the land was too heavily timbered to be farmed and too far from existing settlement.

Newspaperman Eric Nichol, chuckled, "The general feeling at the time among their acquaintances was that the 'three greenhorn Englishmen' had squandered their grubstakes. It was said that the government polished up the chunk of coal in the New Westminster shop window in hopes of bagging another clay pigeon."

Two decades later, this kind of scepticism had infected the influential London Truth Newspaper that ran the following editorial, "British Columbia is not worth keeping. It should never have been inhabited at all. It will never pay a red cent of interest on the money that may be sunk in it."

In actual fact, the three really were naive greenhorns who were staring at a fortune in timber that seemed like an impediment to the building of those neat little rows of brick houses they remembered in Salendine. They literally could not see the forest for the bricks. Where cheap lumber abounds, nobody is going to buy expensive bricks.

On November 4, 1862, undaunted by the derision, the three men were hard at work clearing a cabin site on the bluff. The erection of that first cabin, long known as "Morton's Shack," was a task of considerable fortitude. Yes, at last, Vancouver had a name. It was called Morton's Shack.

The men had limited tools at their disposal and began the work with an audience of curious natives who, draped in their woven blankets, watched every move the trio made. Some were half hidden behind the trees, others gazed openly as the cabin took shape. Morton and his friends worked with an eye to the task and an eye to the audience. They had heard tales of torture and scalping in the American West, and while these tales had no place among the Indians of the West Coast, the Yorkshire men were still subject to the doubts of a runaway imagination that would be common to any newcomer.

One day a native showed up with a Salmon looking for a sale. Brighouse couldn't understand his Chinook and called on Hailstone who was just as much at a loss as Brighouse. Finally Morton appeared while the Indian kept repeating "sit-cum-dolla hiash close." That there was a fish for sale was obvious, but Morton said, "No!" When he returned inside he remarked to the others, "Imagine six dollars for a Salmon and all my clothes." He had it wrong. The Indian was telling them the fish was theirs for fifty cents. A year would have to pass before John Morton could understand Chinook. With today's prices that fish would have been worth a hundred dollars.

An amusing story that Morton related to his son tells of a young Yorkshire man by the name of Jim Holroyd who came to live with the trio. Holroyd knew nothing of Chinook, but had read a great deal about the scalping proclivities of the North American Indians.

Joseph Morton recounted, "There was a grindstone set out in front of the cabin for grinding axes and tools, and as my father and the others were very friendly with the Indians, the Indians were allowed to use it, a privilege which they appreciated. Early one morning before anyone was out of bed a noise was heard outside the cabin and Holroyd asked somewhat anxiously, 'What's that? What's that?' Father replied, 'Don't pay any attention; I expect it's some of those natives around. Go back to sleep.' But no more sleep for Mr. Holroyd if indeed, Indians were in the vicinity. He got out of bed and got ready for action. He opened the door about an inch, peeped out, and saw the ugliest-looking Siwash with an axe in his hand standing beside the grindstone. The Siwash grinned, which made matters worse; it was enough to scare any greenhorn from Yorkshire. Holroyd slammed the door and bolted it and called out to Father, 'Indians, John, and they've got their tomahawks and are ba'an going to scalp us.' Knowing that there was no danger, Father smiled and said to Jim, 'They're only there to grind their axes.' But Holroyd was not so sure and had made up his mind that there was going to be no axe grinding by savages while he was lying in bed. His faith in Father's assurances was completely outbalanced by the blood-curdling yarns he had read. He got quite excited and said to Father, 'What have I got to say to those fellows? They've got to go.' Father said, 'Open the door and say "Mika Clattawah," which in Chinook means, "Go away."' Holroyd opened the door about one inch, peeped through the crack, and roared with the full force of his lungs, 'Michael, Clatter away, damn thee.' The Indians enjoyed his speech immensely; they grinned still more and went on grinding."

Morton would spend seven years in that shack, relieved by Hailstone and Brighouse as each took their turn to keep their grubstake current. One day they received visitors. Two native women and a warrior dropped by. Since neither Englishman knew Chinook, the enthusiastic warrior wasted a lot of breath trying to convince the two white pioneers about something that neither of them could understand. Meantime the two women proceeded to jump over a bench they found, which Morton thought might be a dance. With increased frenzy the women continued to jump the bench while the message being delivered to them by the warrior went over their heads. The now thoroughly entertained Englishmen were nonplused when their visitors left. None the wiser, the pair checked the scene out with their friends in New Westminster. Apparently the point of the exercise was to show that here were two women who had the strength to work, and to work hard. Was employment their only motive? Perhaps, but mixed marriages between native women and pioneer men were not uncommon. None of the Yorkshire greenhorns ever showed any interest in this. In any event, whatever was being offered was declined and the whole episode was stored in Morton's mind as another one of those hair-raising tales that he was famous for—both in Vancouver and in England.

With time on his hands, Morton cast curious eyes on Deadman's Island and explored it at will. Brighouse suggested that the island could be purchased for five dollars. The lure of empire! A seed had been planted.

Chapter Eight
Morton's Shack

Vancouver's first house was built in the fall of 1862. Shortly afterwards they built a barn on the bluff overlooking the Burrard and cut a trail to False Creek. Then came the non-offer of a lifetime. Blinded by the desire to clear the land, a businessman offered the greenhorns a few dollars to lease their property and remove the trees. Talk about luck! Naturally the greenhorns took the offer only to discover a few years later that they had given away a fortune. As the trees disappeared the next most exciting thing in their lives came in 1867 when Jack Deighton arrived. "Gassy Jack" Deighton was born in Hull and has the distinction of building the first saloon. Contrary to public myth, he was only one of many newly-arrived. Morton's settlement was first and had already begun—even though it was only a shack, a barn, and a trail. The men spent their first Christmas that year in New Westminster. When, three months later, the Royal Engineers made their first survey of the area, Lance Corporal George Turner wrote across the plan, "Brick makers' Claim." Wrestling with the strange new environment the trio struggled along in their new home, doing a little clearing and working by turns for their grubstake, either in New Westminster or Victoria.

Shortly after they had completed their cabin, the claim was disputed by Robert Burnaby, who cited an earlier filing. Hailstone and

Brighouse might have yielded but Morton was in no mood to give in so easily. Judge Brew, not informed of Burnaby's name, is alleged to have pronounced the claim written by "either a liar or a knave," an opinion Morley comments on as "hasty and unduly acrimonious—obviously out of character with Brew's usual manner."

Such as they had, the natives kept the trio well supplied in fish and food thanks to the privileges of the grindstone. For other groceries they walked to New Westminster and returned with laden packsacks. Morton always enjoyed meeting the Indians[10], though at times they caused him problems. Early in the year some stole tools. The three men in turn filed a complaint with Colonel Moody of the Royal Engineers who called old Chief Capilano into New Westminster and gave him a talking-to which, in Morton's understatement, "prevented any further trouble."

---

10   I am well aware of the rights of the indigenous people who despise the Indian nomenclature, however for nearly two hundred years in Canada and four hundred years in the USA, Indian was the name for native people. I respect their wishes but cannot write history without using *Indian* as a word.

Colonel Richard Clement Moody

Another colourful story related by Joseph Morton about his father is as follows: "One morning he was aroused from sleep—he was alone at the time—by a wrackedie shindig outside his door. Listening, he made out that it was the noise of Indians, and he thought for sure they were going to clean him off the Inlet, scalp him, kill him and do something to get rid of him. He slipped out of bed and dressed quickly, put his gum-boots in the bed and covered them up, and, arranging the bedclothes to make the bed look as though it was occupied or someone sleeping in it, sneaked out into the bushes to await developments. Nothing happened, but the big shindig continued in full force, kyhying, jabbering and yelling in loud Chinook in a very excited manner. Then, out of curiosity, he went through the bush to investigate all the excitement.

"Going down to the head of Coal Harbour he saw there a great crowd of Indians excitedly dancing, throwing up their arms, and yelling about the place where now is the 'Zoo,' at the entrance to Stanley Park. Hanging to a tree and swinging and swaying, he could see a body, and approaching more closely, keeping well out of sight and well concealed, got so close that he was able to discern that the swinging body was that of a klootchman (Indian Woman).

"His curiosity was satisfied, but not knowing the reason, he immediately headed for New Westminster and reported the incident to the authorities. They in turn investigated and brought some of the natives to Westminster to give evidence. The Indians said that a native woman had killed another woman's papoose and that they thought it was a fit instance in which to exercise the King Georgeman's law, so they had taken her and hanged her[11].

"They were warned not to do it again; that the King George men would attend to that in the future, and that they, the natives, would be severely punished if they took the administration of justice into their own hands."

This author stands amazed that those native tribes who were British Columbia's first inhabitants could so blandly accept the white man's rule of law. I personally suspect that the authority of the gun had something to do with it. On a deeper level, I further suspect that the suppression of native wars was appreciated by the first nations themselves. It must be a terrible life to wake up to a raiding party of a foreign tribe when you least expect it, not knowing what torturous fate awaits you. The arrival of the white man was appreciated in Canada. Not so in the United States, where the lawless west resulted in the death of so many of the original tribes. In the case of Canada, the white man's arrival put an end to the interminable tribal wars that left the indigenous people with only losers. How the Iroquois wiped out the Hurons illustrates my point.

---

11   Amazing! King Edward had only been dead a short time when King George the fourth ascended to the throne. In no time the Indians acknowledged the new king.

Shortly after the pre-emption was granted, Morton had been thinking for some time about the possession of Deadman's Island in Coal Harbour. He was aware of its use by the natives as a burial ground and of the problems involved in gaining possession, however, he was determined to try. He mentioned the subject to Brew, who inquired of him if he realized the nature of his request. Always willing to assist a settler, he asked Morton if he was acquainted with old Chief Capilano. When Morton explained that it was the chief himself that came to his shack to sharpen his knives it appeared to Brew that the acquisition might be possible. A week later while Morton and Capilano were at New Westminster, Brew explained everything to the chief in Chinook. Horrified, Capilano rolled his eyes and cried, "Kamloose Siwash Illahee." By this time it was obvious to all that possession of the Island by a white man was an unthinkable violation for the Indians. Brew informed Morton that he'd better forget the whole matter. Subsequent investigation of the island revealed it to be a sort of burial place with hundreds of cedar boxes tied in the trees with the contents of white bones and tassels of long black hair.

Englishmen understand farming; they practically invented the science. If brick making is to be postponed then why not do the obvious. In 1863 Brighouse persuaded Morton and Hailstone to join him in a venture to lease farmland on Lulu Island, which they worked together. In the following year, Brighouse, who had financial connections in England, secured some 700 acres on Lulu Island. Since someone had to stay back with the cabin, the lonely vigil fell to Morton who still held high hopes for his business venture in bricks. His partners, somewhat reluctant to begin, finally agreed to initiate the venture within the year. Brighouse packed the stove on his back that would serve as a kiln, bringing it all the way from New Westminster—a Herculean task considering the primitive condition of the trail. Later that year the pile of bricks grew but the demand was limited. The inevitable termination of the venture was all too apparent. There was nothing wrong with the enterprise except that it was premature for a pioneer community. The obvious wealth towered above their heads. Unfortunately for the Yorkshire men, their landlocked minds could not conceive of the forest wealth that stood erect soaring into the sky but as already explained missed their golden opportunity.

The "greenhorns" had come to no unusual bounty of wealth. Had they known what others knew they could have amassed an early fortune. Meantime for entertainment they had to content themselves with the news of the world, a modern miracle now made possible because Marconni had invented the telegraph with a cable that linked the New World with the Old. By this means of rapid communication, Morton and his friends knew that the Union armies had won the Battle of Gettysburg within days and could discuss the issues involved. Furthermore coming from the land of the free, they would have approved when the Emancipation Proclamation for the Negro slaves that was affirmed by Lincoln on January 1, 1863. This was the move that both France and England affirmed with dire consequences for the South.. Any hope of recognition of the Confederate States of America by European powers ended when the "abolition of slavery" replaced "preservation of the Union" as the reason for the American Civil War.

Chapter Nine
A Renamed City Takes Off

The first two years around the cabin must have been lonely. According to Morton, in 1864 "things began to liven up a bit." A sawmill was built on the north shore of the inlet; Morton paid $3.00 for the first three hundred feet of wood cut. Short on cash, the greenhorns had already made the blunder of a lifetime when the men decided to lease their land to the loggers. Bricks had blinded their eyes and they were ignorant of the money to be made in timber. It must have been hard to see others harvesting the wealth of the timber, which could have been theirs. They were indeed three British Greenhorns. Five years later, when in 1867 the land was secured and our pioneers still poor, Brighouse farmed on Lulu Island. Morton and Hailstone worked where they could until 1879 when they gave California a try looking for employment; a ritual followed by thousands of disappointed gold-seekers.

 It is one thing to be wealthy and another to be land rich. The greenhorns were in the latter category although Brighouse with his British connections fared better with farming on Lulu Island. A man with money was John McDougall who took the contract to clear the west end of stumps for the CPR. The greenhorns (probably with a swap of land) agreed to a contract to have their land cleared as well. If left alone, McDougall could have made money but he made the unfortunate choice of hiring Chinese immigrants to do the work at half the white man's salary. With 400 workers tented down and succeeding to get the job done, all was well until a unruly mob of unemployed whites stormed the camp, burned the tents and drove the Chinese workers out of town. Vancouver in 1867 was not an example of good race relations. Today as a cosmopolitan city of Oriental and Caucasian peoples, it is a model of multiculturalism success.

Morton's shack survived the riot but not for long. Eventually the lease holding loggers gave up any attempt of protecting the evidence of the white man's construction. Its value was negligible. The old shack was still standing in 1879 in disrepair and overrun with wild currants, raspberries and Foxgloves blooming in the summer sun until the Indians finished it off. Leaving the unguarded shack to Indian pranksters, the absence of white settlers was celebrated by burning the shack to the ground.

Meanwhile, over the years, the timber barons continued to harvest a fortune from the Brick Maker's Claim, including the largest tree ever felled in the Vancouver area. It was over 350 feet high and the trunk nearly 16 feet thick.

The Greenhorns looked at their forest and wondered how they could clear the land

In 1864, Captain Edward Stamp arrived from Port Alberni and built hid sawmill on the south side of the Inlet. This mill, which began to produce in 1867, became the Hastings Mill. In 1865, for a truly brilliant stroke of financial acumen, Jerry Rogers, also from Alberni, set up a camp to produce spars for shipment to the boat builders of England and Australia. His camp was situated on the south shore of English Bay by a little cove where the Jericho Country Club now stands. The name "Jerry's Cove" was later transformed into "Jericho."

You can't call a burgeoning village "Morton's Shack" for long. As colourful people started to arrive, as already alluded to, an enterprising pioneer named John Deighton was enjoying pioneer prosperity: Jack Deighton's Saloon! No one could excel him for a tall story. In short order the house-building locals solved the name problem by immortalizing John Deighton with the title of *Gastown* in honour of the fastest gums in the west, Gassy Jack himself. Settlers trickled in slowly but steadily to the shores of Burrard Inlet. The biggest news in 1867 was the formation of the Dominion of Canada. Ominously, in the same year, the United States purchased Alaska for $7,200,000 sandwiching British Columbia between. With the ever present American swagger to contend with Morton, loyal Englishman that he was signed with 900 others on a petition originating in New Westminister that British Columbia should join the fledgling nation that now included three and a half million. In 1868 Joseph Spratt arrived with a machine to press the oil from limitless tons of little herring caught in the inlet. Spratt later built a great skew or houseboat aboard which he used to can salmon. This floating cannery was equipped with propellers and engines, and was known on the coast as "Spratt's Ark." For a while Gastown was the infamous name of the now burgeoning community and Jack's saloon was the meeting place.

A sky pilot preaching on the roof of Gassy's saloon

Downtown Gastown was within view of Morton's shack.

Cordova Street in Gastown, 1880s

During those days, the sky pilots would frequent the saloon. Sky pilot was the name the locals gave to the travelling preachers who came by to sermonize the sinners. In those times entertainment was so limited that a good brimstone preacher with a fiery tongue was welcome news. The patrons would clink their beers and surprise everyone by singing hymns with the best of them. As teetotallers, these occasions would be a challenge to the greenhorns, who, even though they were lapsed Baptist churchmen would feel uncomfortable in such circumstances. They wished the sky pilots well (travelling preachers and usually Methodists) but probably declined their invitation to the notorious saloon that they so studiously avoided. No surprise. Churchmen are a breed to themselves and that divide still exists to this day. While they make great neighbours their lifestyle kept them apart. Small wonder that the Morton name was fading around the town that he envisioned and was supplanted by other names like Jerry Rogers and Jim Fraser. To the chagrin of Dominic Charley (a first nations man), Fraser predicted that the white man would overrun the city. I wonder what either man would think today about our cosmopolitan Vancouver.

Given the reputation of Jack Deighton, it is a small wonder that today's uninformed man of the street supposes the honour of first settler goes to him. Given the kind of harbour Burrard Inlet provided, Morton thought Liverpool would be a good name for the city he envisaged but he also toyed with Blackpool, thinking of the white sands of English Bay. Dignity required a good name. Nobody would have considered Morton. Some thought the name should be Granville, which in turn had trumped Hastings and for awhile, was the choice, but the controversy over the name simply wouldn't go away. Meanwhile, the CPR deal, which Morton had so valiantly resisted until he was cajoled to accept, would settle the debate because by this time William Cornelius Van Horne was in charge. In 1886 the CPR announced their intent to bring the Railroad to Coal

Harbour. Suddenly the serious discussion over the name of the burgeoning town had to be settled.

William Cornelius Van Horne

Why not name the new community with a title that recognized the great man who explored it in the first place? The locals would have none of it. People would confuse the name with the Island. Enter the new CEO of the CPR, an Americanized Dutchman. His forbears immigrated in 1640. Van Horne settled the matter at once – the new city would be called Vancouver. Pity the Dutch. On the east coast, New Amsterdam becomes New York. Here was a chance to even the score. Van Kouver's origins are not to be ignored. By the time he captained the ship that made him his reputation, he was thoroughly English but his name was originally Dutch. Was there a little favouritism with Van Horne's verdict? One is left to wonder. One other item of note took place that the west could appreciate— instant access to the world at large. The invention of the telegraph and Morse code had banished the isolation of the west. In 1867 when Canada became a nation on July 1st, the three newspapers of Vancouver (with a population now of 1,000) presented the news the following day.

In a pioneer community, as is so often the case, first timers fade while the vociferous attract the limelight. The greenhorns prove this point. These Englishmen were churchgoers back home who were misfits with the bawdy characters of the Wild Wild West. Small wonder history passes by the retiring kind for the noisy types like Jack Deighton. Brighouse could mix with the gregarious and was by acclamation declared a councillor in 1886, but Morton and Hailstone were quiet men who would be uncomfortable in a pub either in England or in the new world. It was more fun for the rough and ready to cavort with their own kind. Morton the misfit was not disappointed to take a back seat and quite satisfied with his lot.

Meantime, the authentic Canadian western terminus had passed through three names, with the official one to be given when the city was incorporated in 1886. Meantime, to the disillusion of the greenhorns, some were getting wealthy while they could only wring their hands, watching others cash in on an opportunity, that, had they been wiser, could have been theirs. Getting back to those early years, Gordon Elliott writes quoting Grant: "Those were profitable days for hand loggers. The timber, which lined the shores could be felled right into the waters of Burrard Inlet, and the mills paid four dollars a thousand feet for the logs. One man could sometimes make as much as $1,000 in a month or six weeks. If this money was earned quickly, it was spent just as quickly. And 'Gassy Jack' saw to it that he reaped his share.

"Hastings Mill, on the south shore and Moody's Mill on the north shore of Burrard Inlet, became famous throughout the Pacific Basin. Ships from all over the Pacific and from Europe began to enter the harbour. Sometimes as many as twelve or fourteen deep-sea vessels might be seen in the inlet at once, cramming their hulls with the prized timber from virgin forests. Ships require provisions and the presence of so many created a lucrative trade for suppliers. One such person was George Black, a butcher, a man as bright as he was handsome and a man of whom Morton had fond memories. He built a floating wharf down on the waterfront from which he supplied ships with beef and salt salmon. He did a lucrative trade in beef from cattle which he drove up from Oregon."

Like so many before them and so many after, the greenhorns were living proof that experience and opportunity often bypass the labouring man in favour of the person with special knowledge, .plus a little bit of luck.

Chapter Ten
Canada Comes of Age

Morton and his friends witnessed fortunes being made, yet they remained in penury. Meantime, the greenhorns were spectators to one Canadian upheaval after another. Morton's Shack had given way to Gastown. But before Gastown had become Granville, consider these seismic events. To the relief of most of the locals, British Columbia joined Canada in 1871 as a province with less than 10,000 white settlers. In 1873, the Northwest Mounted Police was formed. Yes, they put a stop to the notorious whiskey trade, but the reason they had red uniforms was to distinguish them from the bluecoats of the American army. Fear of an American takeover was still present.

In 1878, Sir John A Macdonald lost his seat in a national election in the east—embarrassing to say the least. How does the father of confederation and leader of the Conservative party solve this one? Solution! Macdonald runs a by-election in Victoria and represents the west when all he knows is the east. By this time, Morton had returned to England looking for a bride. As for seismic events in Canada, he read about it in the newspapers. One year later, the Hudson's Bay Company sold the entire Northwest to Canada for one and a half million dollars. That's more landmass than the Louisiana purchase. Was John Morton witness to all these momentous events? I think so. We lose track of his activities during these days because he's doing what he has to do just to find work on both sides of the 49th parallel.

If hard work and perseverance is the road to prosperity the greenhorns did not lack that kind of opportunity, but in the early days the going was tough. They owned land but were unable to sell because no one wanted to buy – at least not then. They therefore made their living as best they could, and cherished a faint hope that some day their property would be valuable. The first to pull out of the doldrums was Brighouse. With connections in England he had turned his recently purchased lands in Richmond into a profitable farm. Morton, who by now had returned from California, did gardening and peddled milk for a living. Thus as Morley comments, the spotlight fell on others while these first settlers remained in the background. Brighouse was more prominent in Granville affairs. Affable, generous, and well liked, he served as Councilor of Ward 1 in 1868, being elected by acclamation.

On May 20 1867 the pre-emption requirements had been fully met and the land passed into the permanent possession of the three greenhorns, six weeks before confederation; an interesting coincidence that preceeded something far more significant in the east. This was the year in the east a "true north strong and free" had emerged, making a reputation for John A. Macdonald. The Dominion of Canada was born. Had Macdonald been around Vancouver six weeks before the birth of our nation, he would have clinked his glass in the halls of Jack Deighton's saloon for sure. First for Canada and as an afterthought, one for Morton and his cronies.. Eventually he would be knighted by Queen Victoria, creating a curious dilemma for succeeding generations who would attempt to make a souse a likeable hero on the order of George Washington, father of the United States. As a member of the Sir John A. Macdonald Society, I try my best. For this I quote Lloyd Mackey who informs us that in 1888, Macdonald attended an evangelistic meeting held by Methodist evangelist Crossly Hunter and was converted. Something must have happened at that meeting because thereafter, Macdonald seemed to be able to control his drinking habit to a reasonable level.

In four more years, British Columbia would finalize its border, securing for Canada its western frontier and establish the 49th parallel as a permanent divide. Alas, the Americans once again out bargained us. Instead of Point Roberts and its salmon fishing rights becoming politically and geographically Canadian, the 49th gave what should have been ours to the Yanks.

As we have pointed out, during these days, little is known of the activities of these men except for the marriage of Brighouse. In 1872 the trio heard about the beautiful daughter of a Spanish settler, now a widow. As the wife of Captain Thomas Pritchard, she was a "somebody" of note. Everyone knew Pritchard as the captain of a ship that plied the Columbia River, which illustrates the ease with which Americans and Canadians mixed. The 49th parallel was ill defined and neighbours were more important than nationalities. In pioneer days women were in short supply, producing any number of girl-back-home stories, despite Chief Capilano's efforts at mixed marriages. Granville's first census in 1882 lists 144 names—most of them men. Imagine a city with the current population of two million people with so few inhabitants 135 years ago! Back then, Vancouver was growing at the incredible rate of ten persons a year. So, back to our amorous tale: a Spanish widow is available and, to top it off, she is beautiful! This is an opportunity not to be missed. To marry the lovely senorita, the men would be in a race with many challengers. However, tipped off with prior knowledge, the Greenhorns set out to catch a glimpse of the girl. The eligible three were assured of their destination by a house with the tell-tale lingerie strung out on a clothesline. Charitable men, the trio cast lots and Brighouse drew the lucky straw. Just as well as by this time he was better off than his companions. Alas, Brighouse had no progeny; the considerable wealth that he accumulated was passed to a nephew whose only requirement to sudden wealth was to assume the name of Brighouse. Thus by a caprice of fate, Michael Wilkinson had only to add Brighouse to his signature to inherit a fortune.

(Although another inheritance was modest by comparison, I had an uncle who would have left this author comfortable since he had no offspring. Unfortunately he died before his wife, who changed the will in favour of her nephew (a sister's son). To supplement my inadequate retirement, I turned to writing. Had I received that benefit, this book might never have been written. It is helpful to believe in Providence. Makes life much more worth while.)

Hailstone's two daughters were born in England. It's not difficult to understand why both Brighouse and Hailstone never really were quite able to feel like a Canadian the way Morton did. Elizabeth and Joseph were firmly rooted in British Columbia where they were born. Morton's heart was in Vancouver right from the start..

Brighouse worked his land, which now included a dairy farm near New Westminster. No doubt Hailstone and Morton worked for Brighouse during this time; however, both of them moved around wherever work could be found. In 1874 Morton's name appears on the New Westminster voter's list, Burrard Inlet polling division.

Initially the valuable lands of Vancouver's West End had been divided between the three pioneers in equal portions by lot from east to west, giving waterfront on both ends of the property. Gastown, the portion nearest Granville, bordered by Burrard Street, was drawn by Brighouse. The middle portion went to Hailstone, and the last, nearest the Government Reserve (later to become Stanley Park), was drawn by Morton. Hailstone, who seems to have been the grouch, perhaps because of recurring illnesses, could never quite agree that he had the right section and complained unceasingly until Morton, in 1877, good-naturedly agreed to exchange properties. Morton and Brighouse were then able to merge their properties and develop them jointly. Later Hailstone charged that he had been swindled, but the swindle, if indeed it was one, was of his own making. In the end Hailstone benefited equally with the others although, he often complained.

One story has it that Hailstone gave up in disgust and went back to England. If he did, he came back again because much later in a letter to his wife Ruth, Morton complained that Hailstone was "as miserable as ever." However, we are ahead of our story; we have to get Morton married for the first time before we come to Ruth.

Chapter Eleven
The Adventurer Comes Home to Find a Bride

The homing instinct burns strong in every man and John Morton was no exception. After sixteen years away from England, he had saved enough to return to his native shores. In 1877, he caught a ship to San Francisco where he proceeded to book passage on the *Golden Age* an ill-fated ship headed for England and for home. Arriving at the gate he experienced a strange impression accompanied by a chilling sensation that racked his body. He returned to his hotel to recuperate and was soon feeling much better. The following day he was at the ticket gate again when the same experience came over him a second time. For a Christian, this is an experience with meaning. While Morton had not been much of a churchgoer in his pioneer days, Morton and his kind believed that God led them by such omens. The little decisions of life that we so often take for granted were signs of guidance from above. Morton read such events as the will of God for his life. It helped him to accept without bitterness the blundering mistakes that he made regarding real estate. It also reinforced his piety. Morton saw himself as in a partnership with God, with the ultimate goal of character building, not the accumulation of wealth.

Regarding this second experience as a providential omen, he waited for the next ship before embarking for England. Later he learned of the ship disaster that took craft and crew of the former vessel to the bottom of the ocean. This act of Providence gave Morton strong assurance that he had unfinished work to do. Eventually, after Morton had reaffirmed his faith and become a wealthy man, he gave generously to worthy causes well past his usual tithe. When he learned that the North Vancouver Baptist Church was struggling with a mortgage, he simply paid it off for them. He was beginning to reaffirm his faith that made the singing of the hymns he loved so well take on a meaning that might escape others.

John Morton returned to the familiar haunts and sounds of the England he had left as a young man. He renewed old friendships and astonished his family with stories of the new world. Apparently Morton could spin a story filled with intrigue and mystery; a niece once remarked, "Uncle John would tell us blood-curdling stories of his Indian days." He had other stories as well, like the time Hailstone and Morton canoed across the Burrard in search of better poles. They got them back lashed to their canoe, but not before Hailstone took a tumble into the water. If it had not been for Morton's quick work, Hailstone would have drowned.

A most eligible forty-three year old bachelor, Morton the pioneer had at last the time and opportunity for marriage. How John Morton met the daughter of Blackpool's councillor, Joseph Bailey, is a mystery. (Apparently, at age thirty-seven, she was unclaimed treasure, with the reputation of being a sharp business-woman). Meantime, Morton was something of a celebrity that people wanted to meet. Jane Ann Bailey had a privileged background. Her father eventually became the mayor of the holiday town of Blackpool some fifty miles west of Salendine. Today, Blackpool is a famous resort city of 150,000. In Morton's time it had just become a city of 12,000 souls with the right to elect its own mayor. Its reputation was the ten miles of unspoiled beach that made the place so famous, and in Morton's mind, reminiscent of the white sands of Vancouver's English bay. There he found the girl he had for so long dreamed of in the personable Jane Ann Bailey, and the daughter of a prominent citizen at that. Romance! That irresistible impulse that makes the world turn around bloomed and once again two lovers cannot be separated. One wonders what might have gone through the minds of her parents in giving their blessing to such a marriage. After all, this kind of match also meant a separation that would take Jane Ann to the ends of the earth. Love is such a reckless adventure.

On the 23rd of May 1878, Jane Ann Bailey gave her hand in marriage to John Morton. It was an auspicious event that did not escape notice but ultimately meant a tearful goodbye that was the inevitable separation from family. Jane Ann must have been a resourceful person. She was a partner with her brother Sam Bailey, who was a tea merchant in Blackpool—a partnership she maintained even in faraway British Columbia.

Anxious now for British Columbia, John and Jane Ann made plans to return but for one reason or another they were postponed again and again. Then Jane Ann became pregnant, which added another twelve months. Elizabeth was born in 1879. With business concerns mounting, the departure date could be put off no longer. Eventually the Baileys bade a fateful farewell to their darling daughter. As things turned out, they would never see Jane Ann again.

The adventure of a lifetime does not come without a price. If you weren't seasick then your fellow passengers were. Ten days of ocean travel with all its inconveniences was finally rewarded when they reached the port city of New York. John showed his wide-eyed bride the sights and scenes of the new world, beginning of course in Manhattan.

At the port of New York. This type of ship might have been Morton's style for travel

In 1878, Manhatten had emerged as an industrial giant and America's great port of trade. Greater NewYork had a population of over four million which made it larger than all of Canada combined. With multi-storied buildings and overhead railroads, Jane Ann must have thought she had stepped into the next century. One author described New York with eloquence.

"Overhead, electric wires strung from poles formed an intricate web carrying power for the city's lights, telephones, telegraphs, ticker tapes; the wires ran in heavy strands from pole to pole giving New York the appearance of being permanently draped in black bunting. In the evenings, incandescent light poured from streetlamps, from hotel lobbies and the windows of department stores, the individual splashes of light pooling into a pale radiant haze that hung over Broadway from Union Square up to the midtown theater district. In less heavily trafficked areas, tall standards erected in the center of squares threw down beams of light that gave trees an eerie shimmer and turned the metropolis into the black and white of a historic photograph.

From the streets came an incessant drumming of ironstone, hooves pounding on paving blocks. Untold thousands of horses pulled the carts, carriages, hansom cabs, omnibuses, and streetcars of the city. When it rained, the horses' manure slicked the cobblestones with a stinking brown ooze; in drier months the pulverized manure formed clouds of dust that blew through the air to join the blacker smoke produced by the engines of the Elevated Railway. By now Otis had invented the elevator and suddenly New York became the high-rise mecca of the world."[12] Imagine—a city with eight story high-rise buildings, which Jane Ann had never seen before.

By the turn of the century, Morton lived to see rail travel like this.

Next, came the actual train trip to San Francisco, an adventure within an adventure.

Train travel as John and Jane Ann experienced was still developing. This kind of modernity in the last two decades of the 19th century, did not reach Vancouver until the year 1900.

Meantime, John and Jane Ann would have been reading all about the political controversy that was unfolding in the United States. Rutherford Hayes had finally been awarded the office of President in one of the most hotly contested elections the United States had ever experienced. Political aftershocks of the civil war that had concluded fifteen years earlier. As things turned out, Rutherford B. Hayes proved to be just the reformer the South had hoped for with disappointed

---

12   Matthew Goodman, Eighty Days, p. 18

Democrats not so badly off after all. Samuel J. Tilden who had won the popular vote but lost the Electoral College through political shenanigans retired from public life. Talk about grist for conversation and fodder for why the parliamentary system is so much better.

The travels of the newlyweds were now made easier by the completion of the Union Pacific Railroad. They journeyed across mainland United States, which considerably shortened the trip compared to Morton's earlier junket via Panama. First, they crossed the cultured farmlands of New Jersey, then the rolling countryside of Pennsylvania. If Jane Ann knew the scenes of the Lake country of but the Appalachians dwarfed anything she had ever seen before. Next they travelled the flatlands of Ohio where the newly developed towns looked shrunken in size compared with Pennsylvania.

Next came Indiana where the land was flat and virtually treeless leaving the Mortons to wonder why anyone would want to live there. Chicago on the other hand came as a welcome change of pace. It would have been the first time that Jane Ann and Morton had gazed upon a freshwater lake that seemed as big as an ocean. Chicago on Lake Michigan was now a healthy half million people. Morton would have been able to describe to her how he had read in the papers of the fire seven years earlier that had taken out the core of the city laying waste three and a half square miles of metropolis. To give some idea of comparisons, at this time, Halifax was an unimpressive 30,000. Anna Leonowens described Halifax as "not particularly pretty in its architecture and layout—semi-rural, isolated, narrow, dull and staid."[13] Montreal was about the only city of note in those days boasting a population of 200,000. Knowing what awaited his bride, Morton wisely spoke in glowing terms of what Vancouver would *someday* become.

To return to Jane Ann's adventure, next came the endless prairies. Sadly they saw no Buffalo; small wonder the proud native indigenous

---

13   See Susan Morgan, *Bombay Anna*, p. 188

tribes caved in to white demands so easily. Their means of livelihood almost extinct, they were on the verge of starvation. San Francisco was the final destination but not before Jane Ann had seen the Rocky Mountains and their majestic snow-caps. All of this in the breathtaking time of seven days. The last leg of their journey was the steam tramp to Victoria and the yet unnamed Vancouver. John's first journey had taken forty days. Jane reaped the benefit of progress; the second was completed in the rapid time of twenty-five. Then came the shock—a shanty town of 200 on the Burrard. We can almost hear Jane Ann saying, "What on earth possessed me to come to this untamed wilderness."

How Vancouver looked in 1878

A hundred and thirty-nine years ago Hastings (now Vancouver) was the end of the line. Confederation was only twelve years past. The city, which today boasts over two million inhabitants had barely two hundred residents. Rigor was the order of the day and only the fittest were equal to the hardships. Seventeen years earlier Morton had absorbed the shock of Victoria when it was only a shanty-town. Now it was Jane Ann's turn. Bravely, the new Mrs. Morton took up the challenge. Remembering the opulence of home, she must have wondered what on earth had prompted her to go on this wild adventure. Morton proudly introduced his bride to his friends and showed her their new home. One can only guess how the gentle daughter of a Blackpool councillor raised in the comparative ease of England would adjust to her new circumstances. Certainly they were a far cry from the refinement of the old world. Elizabeth Morton's birth had been the usual celebration with all the care one would expect in England. John had caved under the pressure that loving grandparents must have exercised and delayed his return. The Bailey family celebrated and shared that happy time with friends. In stark contrast, Jane Ann's second pregnancy was subject to all the hazards of a pioneer life and its limitations.

Thanks to the newly invented telegraph. Jane Ann could read of the events of faraway England, but local news came first. High on the list was an unknown Metis by the name of Louis Riel. The self-proclaimed leader of the Manitoba Metis had his merits and the sympathy of Canadians until he made the disastrous mistake of executing a lesser-known figure by the name of Thomas Scott. An Indian revolt in the West could not be tolerated, especially when the Fenian rabble (if they could) would annex the West to the United States. The problem was quickly resolved by the Manitoba Act, which made the Red River settlement into Canada's newest province. As for Riel, he escaped the noose and settled for an undisclosed indemnity and a five-year banishment to the US A.

Meantime, Morton assured his bride that better days were coming when British Columbia joined the Dominion in 1871. As for Riel, he was simply another one of those Indigenous stories that Morton could spin to pass the hours away while Jane Ann brooded the arrival of her next baby so far away from the luxury of England. How she must have laughed when she read that John A. Macdonald was sympathetic to the suffragette movement. Pioneer days were hard for everyone especially women. The biggest event of 1880 was the launching of the sternwheeler the *William Irving* that was built right in Burrard Inlet. For one dollar you could travel all the way to Yale. Meanwhile the happy couple could dream about the wealth that would be theirs when the CPR would be built. On Feb. 3, 1881 Jane Ann gave birth to Joseph. Thirteen days later the CPR was incorporated but Jane Ann would never live to see the benefits. Tragically, she was stricken with illness during the childbirth, lingered for two days and died. Today's gynaecologist would probably surmise by haemorrhaging and infection. Her remains were interned in the Oddfellow's cemetery in Sapperton. Her life in the new world had been one of toil and hardship. Unfortunately the wealth of knowledge from Gray's Anatomy written three decades before had not reached the frontier. The usual precautions of cleanliness we take for granted were unknown in pioneer days. In those days this lack of knowledge resulted in a high childbirth mortality rate. Years ago too many young women reaped the consequences of such ignorance. Her death certificate stated the cause of death as humeral Asthma with Emphysema of the lungs; in other words, symptoms of infection.

John and Jane with daughter Elizabeth

For a while the grieving Morton placed his daughter Elizabeth with the sisters of the St. Anne's Convent of New Westminster where the two Elizabeths met. "Lizzie" the nun was to remain a lifelong family friend. This hitherto stranger must have been a good woman. She endeared herself to the Morton family and especially to little Elizabeth. The three-year-old Elizabeth bid farewell to her father while baby Joseph was placed with friends. The Baileys of England, although as tolerant as Englishmen had become, would not have approved. Given the prejudice of Baptists towards Roman Catholics, it was admirable that Morton would turn to the sisters of St. Anne. Perhaps he imagined that a place where Catholic nuns were working their way to heaven might not be so bad after all. The necessities of pioneer life compelled a camaraderie that tore down old-world prejudicial walls.

These were the darkest days of John Morton's life. Things were not going to get any better soon. If Morton ever had an occasion for gloom, it was now, but he did not despair. If God had spared him once from a doomed Atlantic voyage there must yet be hope. There was an inheritance. Jane Ann had been a business partner with her brother in Blackpool complete with a tea warehouse. New British law required that her brother find the money to pay off his dead sister's share. Morton received 700£ worth $3,500 in Canadian dollars. This in turn enabled Morton to purchase a 363 acre farm near Mission for $2,000.

Chapter Twelve
The Canadian Pacific Railroad Barons Steal the West

When Morton heard the CPR railroad was coming, he was ready. The railroad moguls bluffed when they announced that the tracks would end at Port Coquitlam. The announcement chaffed Brighouse and Hailstone who imagined that their opportunity for instant wealth was slipping through their fingers. They were not alone. The citizens of Gastown/Hastings were also chaffing at the news. Greed is a bit short sighted. The farseeing Morton understood the relationship of harbour to rails. Let the CPR pretend; he knew better and called their bluff. He advised his friends to hang tough. The CPR would come begging to buy their land to reach the harbour. The greatest test for the three greenhorns descended like an unwanted storm. The short-sighted Hailstone conspired with Brighouse, who was too easily convinced. "Morton must be brought to his senses," Hailstone railed. The greenhorns must seize the opportunity to increase the value of their land even if it meant ceding much of it to the CPR. To aid in this misplaced strategy, they enlisted Rev. Robert Lennie who had befriended Morton and would prove to be a spiritual mentor. Through his influence, Morton's Christian life had taken on new meaning. Since Morton's recently purchased farm near Mission could not be reached by roads, for the last leg of their journey they rowed up the Fraser in a small boat.

The confrontation lasted two days. Hour after hour, led by Hailstone, the assault against Morton's verdict was mounted. Tensions grew, and finally, against Morton's wise and better judgment, he relented. A short-sighted greed prevailed. The CPR negotiators offered to build the railroad to Coal Harbour, provided the greenhorns would cede 60% of their land to the company. The lure of 220 acres made valuable would be the greenhorns' compensation. In a few years the CPR bluff was understood, but by then it was too late. Morton, the Christian gentleman, had relented rather than risk outright war with old friends. Millions of dollars were at stake. Brighouse and Hailstone were still the greenhorns. Morton was the farseeing sage but he had caved. The unrepentant Hailstone eventually discovered that his strategy was misinformed, but he never admitted it to Morton. These were dark days to be sure. First was the loss of his wife. Now, another bad deal. It was next low point in that heroic pioneer's life. Craigellachie, (just east of Revelstoke) a milestone in the tumultuous railroad history of Canada was a victory for many and it eventually made Morton a wealthy man. Had the greenhorns listened to Morton, they would have been richer by far. Morton took it all in stride and never let it cloud his gentle nature.

Lord Strathcona driving the last CPR spike at Craigellachie - Nov. 7, 1885

Locomotive #374, the first trans-Canada passenger train, arrives in Vancouver, May 23, 1887 *34

All this comprehension would come later, meanwhile John continued to farm, living the arduous life of one deriving his livelihood from the soil. Morton had learned by experience that farming in Mission gave a two week advantage in the growing season, making it possible to market his garden produce in Vancouver ahead of his competitors at the best possible price— more evidence of the resourcefulness of his mind.

Chapter Thirteen
The Allure of Romance Never Dies

When Morton acquired his farm, this new venture introduced Morton to Mrs. Mary Ann Trethaway, the operator of a trade-in-store in Mission who was something of a matchmaker. Learning of the widower and his two children, she sent a letter to Mary Ogle, an aunt to a certain young lady by the name of Ruth Mount, an English family residing in Iowa. This letter included an invitation to Ruth Mount to come to Canada for a visit to meet John Morton. I can't imagine such an epistle with such far reaching implications being sent without Morton's approval. What kind of dreams does a man have having known romance to see it taken from him. So was it the joy that inspires us by that special woman that we long to love or was it the practical need for a partner to raise two children while Morton attends to his farm? Or perhaps a little bit of both. One thing we know; we were made for love and John Morton was no exception. Ruth Mount now becomes the equivalent of a mail order bride.

Can you picture in your mind what a thirty-six year old spinster would think receiving such a letter right out of the blue. Perhaps it was something like this, "Don't know who this John Morton guy is, but nothing ventured nothing gained." Ah! The necessities of Pioneer

Days or the universal longing that is built right into every person that has been born into this world. Here are two people who for starters have one thing in common: they both speak with a Yorkshire accent and share a common heritage. They both grew up in the English Midlands about twenty miles apart. What must Ruth Mount have thought? What's more, our prospective bride had nothing to go on except a matchmaker friend and, as the crow flies, a 1,500 mile trip with no guarantees. To her everlasting credit this daring young lady decided to give it a try. The future "Vancouver Grand Madame" arrived in what was then called Granville, expecting to spend the evening with friends in Moodyville (now North Vancouver), but unfortunately she missed the ferry across the Inlet. Our indomitable lady, unabashed, gathered up her coat and slept the night alone under the trees, at approximately the foot of present-day Carrall Street, and this was early April. I had a spinster friend, who tried the same thing with a man she met via the Internet. Risking all, she flew to Fairbanks, Alaska. The enthusiastic suitor didn't even show up to meet her at the airport. When she looked him up, whatever took place on that epochal day, I cannot relate. Suffice it to say that within twenty-four hours, she was on the first flight home minus the price tag of a round trip flight to Alaska. Our story has a much happier ending.

John Morton and Ruth Mount were married on Tuesday, April 22, 1884. John was fifty years old and Ruth was thirty-six.

Ruth Mount was a tiny woman with doll like features. From the moment John Morton met her he knew that she was for him. Ruth obviously felt the same way, for the courtship lasted a scant two weeks. (Remember when you met that special person and could talk for hours and the day was still too short)? Thus began a beautiful love relationship that was to endear John Morton to Ruth and Ruth to John for the rest of their lives. As a clergyman, I have performed these kinds of marriages myself and even if the bloom of youth has mellowed into middle age, romance is that ever present power that can unite two people into a life of fulfillment that deserves a history like I wish to show to my readers.

The marriage ceremony took place in New Westminster with Rev. Ebenezer Robson, a Methodist minister, performing the ceremony on April 22, 1884, —for Vancouver— my favourite time of year. Whenever friends tell me they are going to visit Vancouver in the summer, I always try to persuade them to go the last week of April when the city is ablaze in spring flowers.. But where in those primitive days do you go for a romantic retreat? The demands of the farm came first and then at last after six weeks went by—at last the happy couple could take their honeymoon. So what is the chosen destination—a trip to old Granville that was still only a village of 400 inhabitants. It must have been a novel experience.

Transportation by stagecoach in early Vancouver

Thirty years after that memorable honeymoon coach ride Rev. Robert Lennie gives a description of travel by stagecoach as it was in those times.

"...we cannot appreciate the difficulty one had when we had to depend upon an uncomfortable stage coach, with sometimes objectionable fellow-travellers. And over almost impassable roads. For considerable time the only way to reach the embryo city was by the Douglas Road and around by Hastings. On one occasion I started on my return journey ahead of the stage. Expecting to board it when it overtook me. But it was so crowded that there was no room. and I had to walk the entire distance. [*from New Westminister to Hastings*] After a time the new road which is now called Kingsway was completed. and I secured a horse and buggy and so became independent of the stage coach. In the rainy season the new road. Cut up by much stage travel. Became at times so bad that my buggy wheels sank almost to the hubs." (Quoted from a tract available in the First Baptist Church Archives, Vancouver, The Early Days In Vancouver, Rev. Robert Lennie)

How to plan a postponed but romantic honeymoon? A new corduroy road had been built from New Westminster to Granville. It was called the Hastings Road and the scenery was mostly stumps from felled trees. Tickets for the stage had to be purchased a day in advance. John wanted to show his bride the white sands of English Bay and time permitting, the original clearing where his shack had been built. Ruth's nephew, Edmond Ogle, met them at their destination. Probably Edmond was Mary (Mount) Ogle's son, which makes him a cousin of Ruth.) With greetings accomplished, it was time for some adventure. What is a honeymoon without a romantic boat ride? (Native technology had by now created canoes that could move a ton of freight. Canoes abounded large and small but the only boat Morton could find was a leaky rowboat borrowed for the occasion. When it failed to prove seaworthy, the couple contented themselves with sitting on the beach. In romantic solitude? Oh no—Edmond Ogle was right along with them.

Somewhere in the vicinity of what is now Water Street, for their amusement they watched a few pigs rooting in the foreshore for clams while crows hovered overhead looking to pick up the leftover pieces. (Now a word on behalf of the pigs: we moderns have no idea how important pigs are to a pioneer community. With no garbage pickup, pigs are the sanitary engineers, cleaning up every scrap of refuse. Seems they don't know the difference between a rotting fish head or human excrement. A pioneer village could not survive long without them.) Apparently the day wasn't long enough for Ruth to see the original settlement and she never did get to see that very special historic site until after it was built over with streets and houses. As the day wore on John took his new bride to George Black's for dinner. I guess if you run a butcher's shop the next thing you do is open a restaurant. George Black was an enterprising guy who arranged horse races along Hastings Street when it was only a mud trail. Everybody knew George Black and liked him.

Morton was sure that God had sent Ruth Mount. It was God's arrangement, and Morton was only too happy to comply. With a hardworking wife by his side, Morton now felt secure in his recently purchased farm near Mission with access to the Fraser River. After three years of being without—Elizabeth and Joseph had a mother. Oh yes, of other concerns, in 1884 the bill to extend the vote to women was easily defeated in the House of Commons. John A. Macdonald knew full well it would fail, but what a grand public relations venture for his Conservative government to enlist the support of women who might instruct their men folk how to vote.

Morton had a knack for picking special dates. While he and Ruth were enjoying their junket to English Bay another special event was taking place. Gabriel Dumont, Michael Dumas, Moise Quellette and James Isbister were making a visit to Louis Riel in Montana. Riel recognized it immediately as a call from God in heaven that a new nation should be set up in the West and he (Riel) was chosen to be its prophet. This new nation would be comprised of the Metis nation and the millions that would clamour to join. The pope in Rome would be invited to rule from his new Vatican in a Roman Catholic French Speaking nation carved out of the Prairie wilderness. The venture ended abruptly with Canadian troops shipped West from Ottawa. Next came Riel's death as well as others. This grandiose venture bore the name of the North West Rebellion. It couldn't have come at a better moment for Sir John A. Macdonald. The CPR was verging on bankruptcy and needed yet another bailout from Ottawa. Twenty-five million dollars more for a government already too deeply in debt was the CPR's *impossible dream* as even Macdonald's backbenchers threatened revolt. Then came Louis Riel and his North

West Rebellion. Macdonald made the most of it to accomplish the railroad miracle. The House of Commons voted the money to defend the country in a time of rebellion.

There was however a problem to overcome. How can you ship an army west with an uncompleted rail line, which peters out in Northern Ontario. Riel was no Muhammad warrior. Had he been decisive, he might just have given Ottawa a very rough ride. Unfortunately for Riel, no heavenly angels came to his rescue and while he dithered Macdonald acted. The incomplete railroad to Winnipeg was assembled in less than two months to transport an army of 5,000 and the retribution was swift.

The political price was the alienation of the province of Quebec who sympathized with the French speaking Metis. From now on the French voted Liberal instead of Conservative. In the end the overwhelming English-speaking Canadians prevailed. Louis Riel was captured, put on trial, convicted and hanged. Not all English speaking intellects agreed. Halifax resident, Anna Leonowens, the internationally known writer and lecturer sided with Riel.[14] (Anna would become better known after her death when the fictionalized movie, Anna and the King of Siam made her famous.)

For John Morton and his newly married partner Ruth, the story must have been riveting news now that the telegraph could inform the local newspaper. How could they have learned all this? Thank Samuel Morse for inventing the telegraph. From 1844 onwards, the news of the world was available to the progressive West starting with the weekly newspapers. Chapter 13 Vancouver Burns to the Ground

Can't you see the Newspaper headlines?! What a year 1885 turned out to be. Vancouver was at last experiencing a population explosion reaching the unheard of number; 3000 residents. The building boom was on, but the CPR railroad company was broke and Parliament was

---

14 See Susan Morgan, *Bombay Anna*, the Canadian Grande Dame, p.186 & ff.

not about to loan another $25,000,000 to the money-pit CPR but as we have already explained, the Duck Lake battle changed everything. Fought in Manitoba between the Canadian government and the western Indian Alliance of Cree and Metis under Louis Riel had unwittingly rescued the railroad. The outcome determined that the west would not be French and Roman Catholic. It was the Plains of Abraham all over again. The ghosts of Wolfe and Montcalm are still at it and the French came off second best. This is the kind of news that the Mortons and their friends would have discussed for years.

Then there was the perennial threat that the Americans who subscribed to Manifest Destiny (meaning that Canada was to be annexed by the USA.) that was always lurking in the shadows. English speaking Canada prevailed—the unfinished Railroad that was needed to transport the army to put down the rebellion taught the Americans that Canada was a force to be reckoned with. With the CPR government backed loan, the railroad clawed its way through the Rockies. The thin steel line of transportation connecting the loosely aligned peoples of Canada not only saved the nation from the Americans, it also silenced dissent. Canada would be British. This was the unfolding drama that made for such fascinating reading. The newly married Mortons must have marvelled at the news that had undertones for their future destiny. But now it is time to draw attention to the untamed West and the city of Vancouver.

One year after the astounding news of the Louis Reil rebellion, just as things seemed to be settling down came what must have seemed like the crises of a lifetime. June 13, 1886, John and Ruth Morton looked at the setting sun trying to understand the strange plume of smoke that dominated the horizon. They would not be long in learning that fire had broken out in Vancouver where workmen were blasting stumps. Soon it was a raging inferno, whipped and driven by an abnormal blast of summer wind. Desperate men vainly tried to stave off the fire above the corner of Cambie and Cordova Streets. Chunks of flaming wood were flying clean over their heads and dropping on the frame buildings of old Granville. Father Clinton, the Anglican Rector of St. James Church, rang the church bell vigorously as a fire warning. Five minutes later the flames lashed down the wooden sidewalk in front of the church. Minutes later the edifice was in flames. From street to street the fire progressed unabated. It was hopeless; the recently renamed city was doomed. In less than an hour, Vancouver had burned to the ground. Well not quite—an hour later, there were still four houses standing.

Edmund Ogle opened his store one week before the fire.

The morning after the June 13, 1886 fire.

That same morning, as far away as Mission, John and Ruth Morton had seen the sky turn an ominous black as the smoke clouds darkened the sky. News spread that 3000 people were homeless, and the entire province was in shock. Naturally, Morton wondered what this would mean for him. Forty people perished but Morton's friends survived. On a daily basis every town needs to eat, but with a city in ruins, Morton's produce was needed now more than ever. Being the caring churchman that he had now become, Morton swung into action. He, along with many other surviving neighbours, did what they could to assist and provide. Among the burnt out storekeepers was Ruth Morton's nephew, Edmond Ogle, who had opened his new dry goods store one week before the fire wiped him out.

To become a great city, a metropolitan area must go through four generations of architecture. The shanty-town comes first. A more substantial town comes next. Masonry comes third. This endures a lot longer until even these buildings are demolished for the lasting structures that appear in photographs. Some might say that Vancouver is well past that generation and is now in the fourth generation. Vancouver is the Western Jewel of Canadian cities, the pride of its inhabitants, and a picturesque wonder to the world. To revisit that incredible year of 1886, it is interesting to note that from that time afterward, many of the new structures were built of brick in defence of fire. Irony! Morton the brick maker was now a farmer. Another "might-of-been" situation had come and gone.

Incredibly the City of Vancouver was rebuilt in a year. Tribute to the ingenuity and motivation of its citizens, who now understood their destiny as a world-class city. On the fateful day of November 7, five months after the fire the CPR was officially completed. Six and a half months later the ceremonial train arrived at Vancouver. Morton standing on his Brickmakers claim with his beloved Ruth witnessed the miracle that would ultimately make him wealthy. One can see Morton smiling on July 30 as the first tea train left Port Moody for the East and further on to New York. Vancouver as he always knew was going to be a boom town. August the 13th saw the Prime Minister himself in British Columbia as Sir John A. Macdonald participated in civic events of significance such as the completion of the Esquimalt to Nanaimo Railroad. One month later the CPR made the telegraph available to the general public with over a half a million messages in the first year.[15] The land poor/rich Greenhorn immigrants were at long last about to cash in. The rush on land sales made the Morton's enough cash to consider privileges available to persons of means. The city that now boasted 5,000 residents beckoned Morton to return to his original investment. Tragedy made him delay.

Morton was still on the farm when; the riots over the Chinese immigrants broke out in 1887. Things got so bad that the province suspended the Vancouver City Charter on February 24. Vancouver was divided into two societies, the civil and the rowdy. On September 27th, after things settled down, the civil society invited the new Governor General, Frederick Arthur Stanley to officially be present as the park that now bears his name was dedicated. At last it was time to take up residence where his future and fortune lay. The ever-cautious Morton would wait five more years.

15　Alexander Begg, *History of British Columbia* pp. 190, 191 The Telegraph had already made it to Victoria and to the newspapers of the day. Widespread information came after 1886.

John Morton with his beloved Ruth with Elizabeth and Joseph.

Chapter Fourteen
England Bound

As sales from the lands increased, affluence came at last to the Morton household. With affluence came time for leisure and memories of England. Was it the eternal yearning in every man's breast to return to one's roots for awhile, or the prejudice that education in England was better? Who knows? In 1888 the whole family went to England where Ruth and the children stayed for four years. During this time Elizabeth and Joseph went to a proper school and were able to go to the Baptist Church in Salendine Nook under the able ministry of Rev. John Thomas. People crammed the English church so much so that an enlargement was underway, which would eventually bring the seating capacity to 900. In an age when there was no radio or television or theatre, Sunday evening church was entertainment par excellent. Gas lighting that could take a darkened auditorium and make it bright as day gave the churches a much needed boost. Once a week the attendance at any church was capacity. Sunday evening services was the morning congregation plus twenty percent. Small wonder the churches were so well attended. There was nothing else to do.

Understandably, Morton's thoughts returned to his beloved Vancouver; there must be a Vancouver counterpart to the church in Yorkshire that he loved. After two years Morton reluctantly returned to Vancouver alone.

He arrived in New York, which he called "all noise and bustle," on June 11, 1890 at 9:00 PM. The next night at 6:00 he caught a train for Ontario. For the first time ever, Morton travelled the all Canadian route and saw what frankly has not changed much over the last 127 years. (I first saw it by train window in 1947).

He wrote to his wife from Vancouver on June 24. The letter is addressed to "My dear wife" and is signed "your loving husband, John." The body of the letter reveals their mutual devotion: "It is the first time since we knew each other that we have been separated so far apart but in heart we were never more united though the distance between us is great. We had a pleasant trip across the Atlantic...we landed at New York on Wednesday the 11th and stayed on board all night Thursday. I went and got my ticket for the C.P.R. They sent me to Ottawa and from there I started my overland trip at 12:20 at night. I went straight into the sleeping car and went to bed: We had a pleasant trip across the mountains, the line is in first class condition and I never in all my life enjoyed a better health than I have done all the way. I never missed a meal all the way and everything went well from beginning to end with the exception of a ... short piece washed away from the track, called a washout. It was on a mud flat between Ottawa and New York. We were detained a little; they transferred us in wagons to where the line was good, reached Ottawa Sat 14th and Vancouver the 20th, Friday." I am especially charmed by the conclusion of one letter that reads, "and now my little dear, I will try and soon be back with you again. I can look forward to the meeting with as much pleasure as you can. Believe me," and as he always so affectionately signed, "your loving husband, John." Anyone who has done this can appreciate Morton's experience. .

Over the year of separation, Morton wrote often and was receiving letters from his children and from his wife, his "little dear" (indeed she was little, but John himself was also short). He was especially pleased by the progress his children made in their schooling. His letters to Ruth include such homely material as that they were "having hot weather," that "the grain is ripe," that "most of the hay is got in very fine order," that "things are rather slack out here just now" that "fruit is abundant" and that "apples, pears and plums were selling at six cents a pound in the shops." The last paragraph of one letter was about the churches, of which he would write about in his next letter. Unfortunately, the subsequent letter is not among his remaining correspondence, but the comment does indicate their interest in the news of the Baptist Churches, which required a separate letter.

Ever a man to care for his own, John Morton would not let Ruth return home alone. After a year, he returned to England where he remained with his family twelve months before personally escorting his family back to Mission in 1892.

John Morton farmed until 1894, selling his vegetables and dairy produce to Vancouver residents. That was the year of the great Fraser flood which ruined farms, drowned animals and washed away 41 miles of Railroad track. It took forty-one days to restore the CPR Railroad. The water level at Mission rose 26 feet. Morton's farm was spared but the lower Fraser was devastated; especially around Chilliwack. Years later flood control gates have eliminated such disasters the last one occurring in 1948. 1894 was also the year that the sternwheeler William Irving was wrecked. Irving had been the most successful of the ship captains in the Fraser trade vessels that mastered British Columbia's most famous river. His home in New Westminister is now a tourist landmark. Testimony to the prosperity he enjoyed. Although he had been dead for twenty-two years when the sternwheeler that bore his name went down, at the time, Irving was still a legend that would have touched Morton in his inaugural year of the city that made Morton's fortune. The irony of Morton's career is that he came to British Columbia seeking gold and like thousands of others found none. One year after he finally made Vancouver his home, gold was discovered in the Klondike. Of the thousands that came to the same penury Morton and his companions experienced by this time for the Greenhorns, things had changed. All because they took the time to pre-empt the valuable lands, we call the West End.

How the times had changed.

Correspondence dating from this period indicates that Morton dealt in real estate, took squatters to litigations, and apologized to clients who complained that the butter he shipped them was rancid. His letters also attest that he visited a great many people and that he kept in touch with Brighouse and Hailstone. A letter of July 12, 1896 is concerned mainly with food in one way or another. Later he writes of dinner at the Rands, makes a comment about inferior butter, and ends with a P.S.: "I shall bring a small piece of mutton if I can get it fresh."

Chapter Fifteen
Vancouver is our Home

The turn of the century was to herald amazing sights to behold. Preparatory to all of that was the coming of electric lights in 1887. Two years later Vancouver had a hospital. By 1894 the population had grown to 13,000, with over a 1,000 Orientals in Chinatown and was growing fast. Five years later, was the year that the British Empire established the two cent postage stamp that would guarantee a letter mailed in Vancouver would eventually make it to England in a month's time.

The Capilano suspension bridge had been completed in 1899. A better version of the rickety original is still there to this day. Provided you have the stomach for the task, it is a tourist attraction to experience. With dizzying heights and vistas to see, I can't imagine Morton not wishing to give it a try. That's not all. The Klondike gold rush had been in swing for three years with 100,000 men traversing through impossible mountain trails to find Eldorado. In 1896 at 30,000 Dawson City was the largest city west of Winnipeg and north of Seattle, surpassing Vancouver in size. As is always the case only a handful got rich. Today Dawson City has a population of 2,000 and a gilded reputation that only the imaginative can appreciate. In my mind's eye, I can see Morton with a little chuckle thinking, "Let them try, they'll soon learn the lessons we learned before we turned to better things." Morton was now thinking of better things. It was time to take up residence in Vancouver. Admittedly, Vancouver was booming but I'm sure after the isolation of the farm, with his renewal of faith, Morton was looking forward to his involvement in the Baptist church he loved and appreciated.

Vancouver in 1899

The other side of Vancouver was more like this

The children were grown and opportunity was knocking at their door. The Mortons moved back to Vancouver in 1894, five years later in 1899 they set up housekeeping at 1151 Denman Street in one of two identical green houses. It was the second time that John Morton had lived in the area. The first time he was a pioneer settler; the second time he was simply another citizen of an already established city approaching 25,000. The land boom was on and Morton still owned land and needed to be where he could manage his business. I like to think there was also the spiritual motivation. Since 1886 Rev. Robert Lennie had become a mentor and friend. Morton's earliest memories were stirred anew as he reflected on the spiritual heritage of his youth. Out of nowhere, Morton became a benefactor of Baptist churches. With affluence and privilege, Morton lived modestly and gave generously to the Baptist cause.

It is easy to offer hindsight observations, and one finds it difficult to resist the temptation to speculate. Even after the uneven CPR deal, had Morton made only a few decisions differently, he might have died a multi-millionaire. His knowledge of brick making was providentially his passport to the wealth he accumulated, yet his fixation for bricks blinded him to the greater wealth of the forest, but it was all downhill after that. For example, in 1884 shortly after the greenhorns had leased their land to loggers, somebody made a handsome profit in fir beams. Huge, knot free beams 34 metres (112 feet) by 70 centimetres (28 inches) square were shipped to Beijing from Burrard Inlet sawmills. They're still there, part of the Imperial Palace in China. Meanwhile when Vancouver had a population of 3,000, flyers advertising "Brighouse Estates" showed up in Arizona. Americans with a background of logging made vast fortunes in B.C. forests, but Englishmen with a background in farming, coal, and pottery saw only the forest as a barrier to settlement. Without the ability to recognize the possibilities of the forests, they had leased their land to others while in vain they sought for gold. It must have been a galling experience to see how easily the hand loggers had made a handsome profit cutting down the shoreline trees. How easily they could have done the same. The decision on the railroad deal depleted their property and cut their returns in half, but for all of this, Morton harboured no regrets.

Waiting to take on lumber at Moodyville wharf, c1872*42

Despite errors in judgment, Morton was, in fact, comparatively well off. Fortunately he had retained some of his land for higher prices. He owned and operated the Morton Apartments, a hotel near the English Bay beach, and built several cottages on his own land overlooking the bay. He was a part owner in the Old Horse Show Building, erected where he had driven his first stake. But my favourite story is how at one time he operated a small herd of ponies for children to ride; it was a familiar sight to those who frequented the beach. Fortunately for Ruth, from time to time he would put property in her name so that when the debacle over his hotly contested will depleted his estate in favour of banks and lawyers, Ruth was sufficiently well off to the end of her days. Morton did not live to see the completion of the Panama Canal in 1914, but before he passed away he would have known that its completion would compound the vitality of the "New Liverpool" that he envisaged half a century before. Vancouver would reap an enormous benefit with the completion of the Panama Canal.

Morton started out in life like the rest of us do. He had some knowledge but more of the rustic type. He was not a big time entrepreneur. He understood risk (not unlike faith). He was willing to believe and risk. Beyond that he was little more than a common labourer who reaped a bountiful harvest. His is an example to the rest of us to accept a little godly discontent to our benefit. Some might say he was lucky. Others like this author might see him as the recipient of Providence. That guiding hand that leads can be trusted to accomplish something significant and well worth while. Not too much success lest we become arrogant: enough achievement to be a blessing to mankind in general and to family in particular. Morton was a Christian role model and a gentleman to be admired.

Above all other social interests, John and Ruth Morton loved the churches that made up the Baptist constituency. He and Ruth attended the old First Baptist church at Hamilton and Dunsmuir. When the First Baptist church finally sold their old building, they relocated to 969 Burrard Street, land that had been a part of the original pre-emption. The lot was purchased for $4,500 with Morton putting up the first $1,000 towards the price. The new structure was dedicated on June 9, 1911, the cornerstone having been laid a year previously on April 2, 1910. Quoting W.M. Carmichael, on that auspicious occasion, "On the platform among the many dignitaries, stood a little, white-haired old gentleman, Vancouver's first settler, who had been a member of the church since its humble beginnings in the little frame structure on Westminster Avenue. Still active and vigorous, he stepped forward and with a silver trowel tapped the stone and said, 'I declare this corner stone to be truly laid.'" What thoughts crossed Morton's mind? It is not hard to speculate; Morton had seen his beloved Baptist church in Salendine expanded and dedicated. In his eyes and ours it was a beautiful structure. Now with those same eyes he would see the Vancouver church he attended surpass the edifice he had known in his childhood for structure and elegance. No, it was not Westminster Abbey, but it was nonetheless a beautiful building, and for Baptist churches in British Columbia, it is still the masterpiece.

The original First Baptist church building, 1904

The new First Baptist church building, 1935

J.Willard Litch, Pastor of First Baptist Church 1904-1907

After the church was dedicated, Morton transferred the deeds of acreage he still held on Dunsmuir Street to First Baptist Church. He hoped it might be the site of a Baptist College but he gave it with no strings attached. The land today would be worth millions, but the church let it go in the depression of 1913 for unpaid taxes. Today it is the site of the Queen Elizabeth Theatre.

In 1911, interviewed by British Columbia magazine reporter J.H. Grant, Morton was asked why he was not richer and he answered in an interesting manner, "Very well, lad, but of course, you know the C.P.R. couldn't afford to come down from Port Moody until my Tillicums and I each donated a hundred lots." Then Grant reminded him that he had much land left to which he replied, "Ay lad, I had." Then without bitterness he gave a hearty laugh and added, "Then, I fell among the forty thieves."

There is perhaps another reason why John Morton did not become a wealthy financier. His outlook on life gradually changed as he grew older. He came to the new world seeking gold. He failed to find it and returned to spiritual values instead. He had experienced despair and remorse in the death of his first wife and in the hardship of a pioneer farm. (His daughter Elizabeth especially remembered the hard work.) His deepening faith in God and his love of the Bible made him evaluate life from a point of view that he remembered from his childhood. He had learned, in short, that "godliness with contentment is great gain." He had enough; why should he strive for more? He was not a hard bargainer.

Tracing the story of the three greenhorns in their later years reveals that a man never quite outlives the longing for home and the scenes that made up his childhood. Morton visited England four times but seems to have loved Vancouver best. In 1903 Hailstone, now a widower, returned to England where he retired, spending the last ten years of his life in Bridlington, Yorkshire, a popular coastal resort even today. After a friendship of forty-one years the Greenhorns were now diminished by one. There is a false tale that Brighouse and Morton outmanoeuvred Hailstone financially and left him poor. Not so. He was worth $500,000 when he died. Sadly it was premature. He fell down a flight of stairs at age seventy and broke his neck.

In 1911 Brighouse, the wealthiest member of the trio, sailed for England for an extended holiday from which he never returned. He died in England vacationing on the Isle of Wight, and was buried in the churchyard of Lindley moor, not far from Salendine. Of the three greenhorns, the sole representative left in Vancouver was Morton.

The trials of John Morton did not end with affluence. His beloved son Joseph did not share his father's faith. Morton's friends described him as "devout," but his son's description was "dour." Joseph's disposition was the exact opposite of his father's. Sceptical, erratic, truculent and argumentative, Joseph couldn't seem to settle down to anything. He put his wife through misery and died in a New Westminster insane asylum in 1933 at the age of fifty-two. John, knowing that his son couldn't handle money, set up an annuity for him in his will. Fifty dollars a month was quite enough to provide in those days. It seems that even Joseph recognized his inability to handle money, as he asked Ruth to split the money between himself and his wife—twenty-five dollars a month for his wife and twenty-five dollars for himself. Those who knew him said he "talked everlastingly for years of how he had been defrauded of his father's estate. First, he claimed by undue influence and designing friends upon his father before death, and fraud and manipulation of the estate by its first executor." It is interesting to note that half of Morton's estate went to his daughter Elizabeth. It appears that Morton had a confidence in his daughter that Joseph could only wish for. Since the Rev. P.C. Parker, John Morton's good friend, was witness not executor, I cannot imagine that the charges of fraud were true. Keeping track of Morton's wealth would have been a challenge for any man because so much of it was still tied up in land. Unfortunately it fell to Northwest Trust who mismanaged the estate and eventually went under in 1915. Joseph's prejudice against the Baptist Church was not without evidence, and can be partly explained by his mental deterioration. The fact that he refused to be baptized tells us he was a nonconformist to his father's ways. Unfortunately, after the collapse of the Northwest Trust, Morton's will became a lawyer's bonanza. The Province Newspaper declared in 1934 that Elizabeth finally received $350,000. Whether she collected that much remains unclear. In 1940 the $100,000 endowment fund for the Baptist Church for education was also contested. How much of that money made it to the Baptist Church remains unclear. As nearly as I can find, $66,000 made it to its intended recipients and the lawyers got the rest. It could not be claimed until Ruth died in 1939. By 1940, the Baptist denomination had split. The older group got $44,000 and the newer denomination called Regular Baptists got $22,000.

    The story of John Morton and his son reveals two perspectives on life that divide so many families to this day. John saw life here on earth as preparatory for the life to come. For this reason, he gave generously to no less than forty Baptist churches in British Columbia. He sent funds for Christian work to India and gave to a ministry that housed children from the slums of New York. I suspect Joseph saw all of this as generosity gone astray. John saw his giving as an investment in eternal values. Small wonder there was conflict.

A happier story is that Ruth who was financially secure had a friend by the name of Mrs. E.E. Buxton of whom we know very little. This special person lovingly cared for Ruth right up to the day of her death. It is pleasant to know that Ruth in her bereavement was not without a companion.

Andrew Grieve with Ruth Morton (centre) and his second wife, Susan

As Ruth grew older she drew great comfort from the ministry of Rev. Andrew Grieve. What pastor Grieve believed was what Ruth Morton believed. In 1922 this confidence would be put to the test. The Pentecostal phenomenon was sweeping the west and evangelist Charles Price took Vancouver by storm. Andrew Grieve's wife was a sickly woman and was especially taken with the evangelist's preaching on Divine healing. Price found a sympathetic pastor with Andrew Grieve and recommended Ruth Morton Memorial Baptist as the place for would-be Pentecostals to worship. The congregation swelled from 250 to 500 and for a while looked like a Pentecostal church in the making. A crisis came when at a midweek meeting Pastor Grieve stood on a chair to adjust a window. He slipped and in the fall broke his leg. Immediately the zealots gathered round and prayed for an instant miracle of healing. When nothing happened others decided to take him to the hospital where the leg was set. Six weeks later Grieve had decided he was a Baptist and not a Pentecostal. The resulting declaration sustained the original congregation and the others left to form what eventually became Broadway Pentecostal Church. Considering how large Broadway has become perhaps this was the best of all outcomes. Meantime, Rev Grieve remarried after his first wife died with Ruth Morton in full support of her pastor's life decisions.

Evangelist Charles Price in action from a Newspaper Clipping in 1922

Chapter Sixteen
Vancouver's Taj Mahal

Four hundred years ago a love legend was planted in India that the world has embraced for fact. As the story goes, Mughal emperor Shah Jahan loved Mumtaz Mahal more than all his other wives. She bore him fourteen children of which seven survived. When she died giving birth to a baby girl, Shah Jahan was so grief stricken that he went into seclusion and fasted for eight days. When he emerged at last, his beard had turned white and he was never the same. He unburdened his grief in building the most beautiful love monument the world has ever seen.

The Taj Mahal was twenty years in building and is made of white marble. It took 20,000 labourers to finish the construction. No record exists of how many died in its erection: probably anywhere from two to six hundred. Supposedly, it was of minimal satisfaction to the emperor, who deemed it an expression of his undying love for the women he loved most. Who wouldn't want to buy into a love story like that? The reality is more likely to be that Shah Jahan was an autocratic ruler flaunting his grandeur and munificence to the world. It is unquestioningly a beautiful building, and a tourist attraction bar none. The love part may have some substance but the myth is probably just a myth.

I would like to propose that the Ruth Morton Memorial Baptist Church is Canada's Taj Mahal with one difference. In contrast to the Taj Mahal, which is a mausoleum, a church building is a people place that is alive with the folks who have called it home over the years. I boldly propose Vancouver has a Taj Mahal that is better than the one that was built by Shah Jahan.

Sixth from the left, Willard Litch now a home missions pastor establishes the Ruth Morton Memorial Baptist Church beginning with a tent

In 1912, Dr. J.W. Litch, who had been Morton's pastor at First Baptist Church, approached Morton about the possibility of endowing a much needed church in the rapidly expanding Vancouver suburbs of which he now was the pastor. Vancouver had grown to a city of 120,000 and was expanding to South Vancouver that had just been cleared of logs for timber. The congregation had already formed but was floundering for lack of funds. Litch wanted it called the "John Morton Memorial Baptist Church" but Morton balked, saying he wasn't worthy of the honour. However, he would agree if it was called after his wife. What a revealing affirmation of genuine love! There are many churches named after famous men that dot our country's church real estate. The Ruth Morton Memorial Baptist Church is the only one named after a woman pioneer. The Taj Mahal myth has a lot of fame but reality is always so much better than myth. At a convenient time, Dr. Litch arranged a tour of the area with Morton. This showing of the building site was accomplished by means of horse and buggy. John Morton never owned a car. Satisfied with what he saw, Morton immediately incorporated the arrangements in his will.

The church was completed in October 1913—exactly 200 years after the letter of application for the Salendine church had been filed by that earlier British John Morton of so long ago. From older pictures it is easy to see that the building bore a modest resemblance to the auditorium of First Baptist before the fire of 1931. (Both church auditoriums have undergone a remodelling and the resemblance no longer remains.)

Pastor Bruce Woods and his wife Joan as Rev. and Mrs. Willard Litch.

Henry and Pat Fietje as John and Ruth Morton. Sunday June 27, 1971 celebrating the famous buggy ride they shared from the west end to south Vancouver when the plans for the new church were conceived. (The costumes we wore were supplied free from Leona Islei's costume store located on Kingsway. She and her physician husband, Henry took a great interest in our production and I made sure that she got credit for that when I was interviewed on CBC.

Our two daughters Debbie and Sara along with Joan Morton (second from right) who came from Salendine Nook to celebrate with us our reenactment. Viola Gleig, (far right) is John Morton's granddaughter. (Note the lump of coal)

*The platform of Ruth Morton Church on Thanksgiving 1916. The lump of coal was to commemorate Morton's discovery of Coal Harbour *50*

Ruth Morton was younger than her husband and John always called her his "Ruthie." Just who conceived of the idea of an expensive stained glass window remains a mystery but thankfully someone decided that this lovely story should be celebrated with this wonderful work of art. In this act of devotion including both building and window, John Morton was declaring his loyalty for the most special person in his life. The rather restrained wording on the memorial stain glass window in the church reads: "This church was built by funds set apart during his lifetime by the late John Morton and afterwards added to by his wife, Ruth Morton, and as a tribute of his regard for her is called the Ruth Morton Memorial Baptist Church." In years to come under the ministry of William Sloan when the congregation swelled to 350, he led the congregation into the building of a balcony to accommodate the increase. Travesty! Over the protests of the loyal friends of the now deceased Ruth Morton, the balcony obstructed the view of the window. With an interior reconstruction project that was completed in 1972, the way was made clear to exchange the West window for the Memorial window (fortunately they were the same size). The new arrangement proved to be much better as the western exposure takes better advantage of the sun. All's well that ends well.

Vancouver's Taj Mahal, Ruth Morton Memorial Baptist Church, 1917 *51

Three weeks after the formal arrangements were made, on April 18, John Morton was dead. His funeral was conducted two days later. The notice in the Vancouver Herald, April 19, page 5, is recorded as follows: "The funeral service will be held in the First Baptist Church on Saturday, April 20, two o'clock PM Rev. Dr. Perry officiating." Friends were instructed to send no flowers.

John Morton had neither the benefit of an education nor the advantage of even limited wealth. In contrast, Brighouse, with access to English financing, built up a sizeable estate. Morton had the vision to foresee the future of Vancouver, but not enough understanding to fully exploit it. He was indeed an English Greenhorn. He was savvy enough, however, to pre-empt the choicest parcel of land in British Columbia and his two friends cashed in on his willingness to share the venture.

John Morton died of chronic bronchitis at the age of 78. Three days earlier the Titanic disaster had occurred. Thus, by a strange quirk of fate, the death of Vancouver's first settler virtually passed without notice. True, both local papers printed obituaries, but they are buried in page after page of accounts of the marine disaster. The unfortunate coincidence diverted the public attention away from Morton and from the many people who could have written stories of inestimable value about this early pioneer. One by one, time has removed the people who might have given us first-hand accounts about him. Sadly, only fragments remain. But perhaps that's as it should be; it is the spiritual legacy that lasts. Morton's legacy lives on in the church that indirectly honours his name. Over the years a few thousand have made this lovely edifice their church, reaping the benefit and passing the legacy on. The list would include many significant names. I list but one who is famous: Terry Fox! And that is another romance story that I will relate in Book Two.

Of the three Greenhorns, Morton was the only one to live out his days in the city that blankets the area he had homesteaded. Brighouse's interests took him to Richmond, where his name is still held in esteem, but he died in England. Hailstone's heart was always in England and to his homeland he returned. It was John Morton who had initiated the venture to the new world, and it was John Morton who discovered and sought out the pre-emption in the name of the three. When they built the cabin, the first house in present-day Vancouver, it was dubbed by the few local residents as "Morton's Shack." Of the three Greenhorns, he alone is buried in British Columbian soil at New Westminster. And in the end, of the three, it was Morton whose name deserves our admiration.

The inscription on the stain-glassed window reads:

This church was built by funds set apart during his lifetime by the late John Morton and afterwards added to by his wife, Ruth Morton, and as a tribute of his regard for her, is called the Ruth Morton Memorial Baptist Church.

By his generosity and concern for spiritual values, John Morton helped to create the church, which bears his surname. It has always been a church active in youth work and has been a centre of foreign missionary activity. Certainly the edifice offers an eloquent way to perpetuate the memory of this pioneer.

When Morton died he left an estate valued at over $700,000, of which perhaps a third went for Baptist charities and education. $12,000 was also set aside for the construction of the church. In this last act of generosity Morton in contrast to Shah Jahan hardly intended a monument to perpetuate his name. He was merely doing another act of Christian duty like so many before of which there are few records. After his death Ruth made her namesake church her own, and she faithfully attended every Sunday.

Four years after John Morton's death and fifty-four years after the coal incident, Ruth Morton, John's widow was attending the church that today still bears the Morton name. It was Thanksgiving Sunday, October 9, 1916. The auditorium was adorned with the traditional stalks of corn and vegetables. That Sunday morning a very unusual object was the centre of the decor. It was a hundred pound lump of coal brought in by one of the members for the festive occasion. One wonders what passed through the mind of Mrs. Morton as she viewed that massive lump of coal prominently displayed in front of the communion table. Need we guess?

From time to time she was called upon for special occasions. In 1932, she was one of ten remaining pioneer survivors "especially invited as representative of bygone days" to witness the opening of the Burrard Bridge. By 1937 she was the remaining witness who had seen Vancouver grow from infancy into a bustling city of 350,000. When I was the pastor of Ruth Morton Church I remember Deacon Jim Wright saying to me, "She always sat in the fourth row and no one would dare to sit there until she had taken her place. She was a delightful person to speak with but until you initiated the conversation she was quiet and quite reserved."

In 1937 Ruth Morton grew philosophical and remarked, "I have lived in a wonderful age. What a period of history! So full of event and invention; chloroform, dynamite, telegraph, telephone, gramophone, radio, bicycles, motorcars, aeroplanes, submarines, the development of the steam and electric railroad, the disappearance of sailing ships and their replacement by ocean leviathans of great power and size; the disappearance of the forest, the building of a great city and the great war." How's that for nostalgia! Alas, she lived long enough to see the advent of World War Two. Ruth passed away on December 14, 1939, at the age of ninety-one. Amongst her letters and notes were the letters that reveal the tender relationship between her and John. Included in one letter was this famous line from Tennyson:

But oh for the touch of a vanished hand
and the sound of a voice that is still!

Today in the Westminster Cemetery the remains of John and Ruth Morton lie side by side awaiting the resurrection. The funeral service of Ruth Morton took place on Saturday, December 16th, two days after her death. It was a well attended funeral that included former mayor George C. Miller and city archivist, J. S. Mathews, who remarked to Miller, "Never again will Vancouver see such a scene as we have just witnessed." To which Miller agreed. A few hours later Mathews would speculate and write for posterity, "Thus from the sight of Vancouver passed the wife and widow of the first white man who called Vancouver his home. Gentle, modest, unassuming, dear little lady, Mrs. Ruth Morton; a pleasant smile, sometimes whimsical, a cheery voice; wife of our first citizen; she whom His Excellency Lord Tweesdmuir Governor-General, sent his good wishes on her last birthday, March 17th 1939, aged 91; she who sat on the log on the shallow strand of shore, now Water street, and watched the pigs rooting clams on the beach, and the crows following picking up the bits; she who, in addressing the City Council last year, said to them 'I think Vancouver is the nicest place on earth'; she has gone to her long home this day, Saturday, sixteenth day of December, one nine three nine, and in this evening of the same day I pay my tribute to the gracious little lady by leaving to posterity my impressions of her passing, and say to them what I know she would have me say. She would wave her hand and smile, and cheerily call

> 'FAREWELL, FAREWELL, GOODBYE VANCOUVER, THE NICEST PLACE ON EARTH.'"

Vancouver's Grand Madame, Ruth Morton

This *nicest place* also became the home of Vancouver's most famous citizen, a guy by the name of Terry Fox. We've already written his story in Book I. This dramatic story cannot be told without the legacy and shadow of the Ruth Morton Baptist church that impacted the life of two people, first Rika Noda and later the young man she brought to church, Terry Fox. This dramatic example illustrates how a past generation impacts the generations to come. We now must pick up the unfinished story of the Terry Fox family.

Some Final
Reflections

In praise of Betty Fox one cannot help but give her credit for raising a son as unique as Terry proved to be. A child's nature and personality reflects the way parents bring them up. Her feisty nature showed up in an indomitable son who against all odds created a Canadian sensation that continues to flourish to this very day. Ask any Canadian teenage highschooler, "Who is Terry Fox?" The chances are pretty good they could tell you. I'm not so sure that they would perform as well if you asked them to name the Canadian Prime Minister he met in Ottawa thirty-seven years ago. At Terry's death Betty Fox picked up the torch and established a commendable legacy of her own. Under the tutelage of the Canadian Cancer Society the indomitable Betty Fox organized what ultimately in 1988 became the Terry Fox Foundation, which as stated before has now raised over $700,000,000 for cancer research. Darrell Fox has succeeded her and siblings Fred and Judith are also involved. As for a lecturer, Betty Fox must have been a good speaker for she has addressed over 400,000 High School students. When the 2010 Winter Olympics came to Vancouver, Betty was selected to be one of the Olympic flag-bearers in the opening ceremonies. If one were to compile a list of outstanding Canadian women, I'm sure Betty Fox would be on the list.

In the last chapter of Book I, I raised the important point of the value of "weakness." I now wish to explain the riddle. Had Terry Fox not failed to complete the Marathon of Hope, I wonder if the annual Terry Fox Run would have arisen. Because Terry Fox was unable to finish the Marathon of Hope others arose to expand the enterprise. Undistinguished admirers of somebody like Terry Fox feel a greater sense of fulfillment when they can participate. Books written to celebrate the achievements of national heroes going from success to success make for dull reading. Why? Because the majority of any populace are all cut from the same cloth and the frailty of human weakness is an essential ingredient. It is out of weakness that we learn humility. Ever talk to a successful protagonist? Boring! Whatever one may think of Jesus Christ, he is the most famous man who ever graced our planet. More people know about him than anyone who has ever lived. Dying on a cross does not seem like a success story. The world has little regard for the shortcomings of weakness, yet it is this very deficiency that has made Terry Fox such a legend. The Terry Fox Foundation is the incredible success story that emerges from what seemed at first to be a disaster. So live your life and accept your failures, this is the stuff of true adventure and a meaningful life.

As the years come and go although destiny has separated the heroic trio, Rika Noda, Doug Alward and Darrell Fox are still the best of friends. All three participated in the April 2017 Royal Museum Terry Fox event at Victoria, B.C. Doug Alward's memorable tribute to Terry Fox on that occasion excelled which underscores the adage, "Don't underestimate the opinions of an otherwise retiring personality." From time to time they still continue to share various opportunities that arise to celebrate the memory of Vancouver's illustrious citizen Terry Fox.

Every Sunday morning across our nation twenty percent of Canadian citizens go to church. They are a creative and inspiring people whose unwritten stories will someday be revealed when heaven comes down to rule on earth. Meantime as we make our journey through time, God's promoted assembly in paradise is now awaiting that glorious day, when time surrenders to eternity.

Since our story concerns Terry Fox, I now wish to comment on his arrival in heaven. The first thing he would discover is "absent from the body, present with the Lord." (II Corinthians 5:8) The Psalmist describes it, "As for me, I will behold thy face in righteousness; I shall be satisfied, when I awake, with thy likeness." (Psalms 17:15) Once again the Psalmist (in this instance it is King David who) writes, "Thou wilt show me the path of life, in thy presence is fullness of joy; at thy right hand there are pleasures forevermore." (Psalms 16:11) After Terry's heavenly arrival, I speculate the following.

Terry fox was thinking, "I wonder if I know anybody around here—well—who are these friendly two persons that are coming to shake my hand."

"Hello Terry Fox, my name is Ruth Morton, you went to the church that was named after me. Come over here and meet my husband John Morton, he was the one who put up the money for that church to be built. The angels have told us all about you so suppose we sit down awhile and have a conversation." Sound reasonable to you? I hope so, because it sure sounds reasonable to me.

Appendix One

To write the biography of John and Ruth Morton without reference to their spiritual legacy would be to leave an unfinished record. As soon as the church building was built and paid for, the congregation mortgaged the place to put up the money for the building of another Baptist church. They carried that mortgage for thirteen years until at last under Andrew Grieve they were able to pay it off. Interesting that Ruth Morton, now a widow, gave a generous gift to make that happen in 1925.

An inadvertent testimony to the character of Ruth Morton appears on the choice of names that appear on Morton's tombstone. Jane Ann Bailey's name appears on the obelisk where the remains of John and Ruth are interred. The decision to include Jane's name on the grave marker is interesting. She was buried in the Oddfellows grave elsewhere at Sapperton. Obviously with Ruth's approval, the mother of Joseph and Elizabeth was given this silent but eloquent respect—a truly magnificent tribute to the heroine of our story.

The church that bears the Morton name also has an illustrious history of very special people who have their own stories. It would be impossible to relate them all but I select just a few that I knew and let them represent the untold story of so many others. Consider Tom Davies, the CEO of Campbell Soups, the Canadian division. Or what about the pastors and missionaries that devoted themselves to ministry? John Ballard, a New Westminster pastor and his sister Leona who went as a missionary to New Guinea. Brothers Gordon Reeve and Richard who became pastors; Dick was a chaplain in British Columbia's penal system. Perhaps the most illustrious of all was Larry Perkins, who is now internationally known as a Biblical scholar. He taught New Testament at North West Theological Seminary and wound up being president. Furthermore he became academic dean of ACTS, (a combination of five seminaries representing two Baptist denominations, the Mennonite Brethren, Evangelical Free, and the Pentecostals). The list could be enlarged but my point is made. Ruth Morton Church has produced an honour roll of achievers and I haven't even mentioned that now lost catalogue of missionaries and pastors who have blessed our nation with their dedication and ministry. I therefore chose to select a few that I knew. Their legacy has blessed Canada with local and international tones.

Appendix Two

The Pipe Organ Story

William Gooch was the organist at Ruth Morton Memorial and until he outgrew the job, his son Eddie had the honour to pump the organ so that his father could play the instrument. (It was his son Eddie many years later that told me this story). William Gooch got wind of a pipe organ that was for sale. He convinced the deacons that this was an opportunity to be seized and the church took up the challenge. The happy result was that the congregation got an instrument that under ordinary circumstances they could never have afforded. When the Victoria Imperial Theatre closed in 1943 that pipe organ was destined for Vancouver. Shame on you Victoria you missed the opportunity to acquire that beautiful Casavant Pipe Organ at a basic bargain price. The bonanza from Victoria was put up for bidders. William Gooch was the winner and played that organ until he eventually turned it over to Herb Hansell. I loved the way Herb who could play by note or by ear could interpret the hymns on that Casavant masterpiece.

Eddie Gooch on his wedding day. Eddie was the source for my information.

Appendix Three

Another Unusual Romance Story from our Church: Dan Fryer and Hilda (Thys) Kramer

Dan and Hilda were teenagers in Winnipeg during the war years (World War I 1914-1918). They were only sixteen but guess what: they fell in love. To their sorrow Hilda's parents moved away to Brandon. Correspondence was not enough for the separated lovers and the relationship cooled. Dan and Hilda went their separate ways and eventually they forgot about one another, married, and settled down. Dan followed a career that eventually took him to the police force. Hilda married a Baptist minister and moved from place to place throughout the prairies. Both had children and both retired to Vancouver. Dan was living at 546 West 13th when suddenly his wife died. Hilda had already been widowed and she moved to Vancouver in order to be near her daughter. Unbeknownst to her, she was living only one mile away from her former beau. Three years passed by when Hilda, needing some groceries, slipped over to the Safeway store to pick up the needed goods.

Providence! Looking to restock some groceries of his own, Dan headed out to the store. A half an hour later, Dan took his grocery cart up to the cashier to pay. Hilda on a similar mission took her groceries to the same queue and was standing next in line. When Dan placed his groceries out on the counter, Hilda recognized him immediately. "Dan Fryer!" she exclaimed, "I haven't seen you in fifty years." His response was immediate, "Hilda Thys! Where have you been all these years?" They both laughed and agreed they ought to have a coffee together and find out. It didn't take long for them to discover that they both had been widowed and were therefore eligible. It was as though it was the year 1918 again when they had kissed goodbye never to see each other for a lifetime. Deja vu! That unquenchable thing called romance bloomed again and I had the privilege of performing the marriage at Ruth Morton Baptist Church, April 6, 1968. I have performed many a second marriage in fifty years of ministry, but I have never seen any second-rounders kiss the way those two lovers kissed when I pronounced them husband and wife. Two more faithful members of our church could not have been found anywhere and I had the privilege of being their pastor for four years until I moved on to my next church in Hamilton, Ontario. Okay, I know what you are thinking. Why this story? Alright! You got to admit romance is a wonderful thing and I hope you get to experience it, however that said, romance is only a picture of a greater love. The Bible calls the church the Bride and Jesus Christ is the groom. When we all get to heaven your marriage is turned into an eternal friendship—not bad considering the glorious future that awaits the followers of Jesus Christ. The love of God is so great that our eternal romance is with God the Father, God the Son and God the Holy Spirit. If this requires some further explanation, we will have to wait until we get to heaven for the full disclosure.

Bibliography

PUBLISHED WORKS

Carmichael, These Sixty Years, Being the Story of First Baptist Church, Vancouver, B.C., 1947

Goodman, Matthew, Eighty Days, Ballantine Books, NewYork, 2013

Kerr, J.B. "Sam Brighouse" Biographical Dictionary of Well-Known British Columbians 1890, pp. 110-113

Matthews, J.S., Early Vancouver Vol 1-7 (2011 Edition), courtesy of Vancouver Archives

Matthews, J.S., Vancouver Historical Journal, No. 3, 1960

Morley, Allan, Milltown to Metropolis, 1969

Nichol Eric, Vancouver, 1970.

Pethick, Derek "The Three Greenhorns," Men of British Columbia, Saanichton, B.B.: Hancock House, 1975, pp.132-137

Ray, Arthur J. I have Lived Here Since the World Began, Key Porter Books, Toronto, Ont., 1996

Richards, J.B. Baptists in British Columbia, Vancouver: Northwest Baptist Theological College and Seminary, 1977.

Woodcock, G. A Picture History of British Columbia, Edmonton: Hertig Publishers, 1980

PAMPHLETS

Mission District Board of Trade, Mission City and District, 1911.

Nicolls, J. P., Real Estate Values in Vancouver, A Reminiscence reprinted as a supplement to A.I.M., September 1962

Northwest Baptist Theological College, Twenty-five Years of Christian Education, Vancouver, B.C., 1970

Grant, J.H. "Burrard Inlet in Early Times" British Columbia Magazine, Vol 7, June 1911

Woods, Bruce A. "The John Morton Story," transcript of the CBC broadcast, June 27, 1971, 10:15 P.M.

UNPUBLISHED WORKS

Vancouver City Archives

Carmichael, W.M., An Autobiography of a Church, compilation of old clippings and archives of First Baptist Church with narrative., 1937

First Baptist Church Archives, Vancouver. See Who was Who in the Pews # 14

Colwell, Gilford, Diary, early member, Ruth Morton Baptist Church.

Gibbord, J. E., Early History of the Fraser Valley, Oct., 1937

Maisey, Murray Archivist First Baptist Church, unpublished material

Mathews, J.S. The first Settlers on Burrard's Inlet, Vancouver, 1932

Matthews, J. S., The Location of Hut and Clearance of the First Residents of Burrard Inlet, 1932.

Mikkelsen, P.M., Land Settlement Policy on the Mainland of British Columbia., 1858-1874.

Morton, John Pacific Press Collection (microfiche)

"Mystery Warning Saved Pioneer from Shipwreck," Jan. 1, 1940

"Morton Will is Contested," May 8, 1940

"Court Rules Legacy to Baptists Valid," Oct. 20, 1941

Vancouver Art, Historical and Scientific Association, "Notes on John Morton," Vancouver: City Archives, add MSS 336, Vol. 41

Cousins, Olive E.J. "A Twelve-Mile Walk Led to Founding of Canadian City"

Huddersfield Weekly Examiner, April 1936

Morley, Alex "Romance of Vancouver Column," Vancouver Sun, April 26 and 27, 1940

Morton, Joseph "Corrections to News Item of 'World' Publication" 1912

Stock, J.H. History of the Salendine Nook Chapel, Huddersfield Examiner, April 18, 1936

"Vancouver's Yorkshire Pioneer Traced" Yorkshire Post, 1936

"Late John Morton Was Old Pioneer" Vancouver World, April 19, 1912

Registry, Vancouver, John Morton Will, May 3, 1913.

Woods, B. A., Historical Journal, Ruth Morton Baptist Church, compilation of old clippings and archives, 1970 (stolen in 1973).

CLIPPINGS
The Files, Archives, Vancouver, B.C.

The Files, Archives, Provincial, Victoria, B.C.

The Files, Mrs. Viola Gleig, granddaughter of John Morton

The Files, Morton Family, Huddersfield, England.

The Files, Press Library, Pacific Press.

The Files, UBC Library

The Files, Special Collections Division, U.B.C. Library

The Files, Church Library, First Baptist Church, Vancouver

PHOTOGRAPHS

The Sundial image in chapter 1, courtesy of George Cunningham and City of Vancouver, Public Art Program, Public Art Registry.

Salendine Nook Church image in chapter 2, copyright Betty Longbottom, licensed under the Creative Commons Attribution-Share Alike 2.0 Generic Licence. The Hamilton Spectator.

Andrew Grieve with Ruth Morton image in chapter 15, courtesy of Ruth Morton Memorial Baptist Church Archives (renamed Mountain Christian Church).

Vancouver City Archives

Unless noted, images used are believed to be in the Public Domain. If you believe otherwise please contact the author.

INTERVIEWS

Mrs. Viola Gleig, Granddaughter of John Morton, Sardis, B.C.

Mrs. Annie Livingstone and Mrs. Edith Paul, daughters of Rev. Willard Litch, former pastor of First Baptist Church and Ruth Morton Baptist Church.

About the Author

Rev. Bruce Woods was the pastor of Ruth Morton Memorial Baptist Church from 1966 to 1972. He was a frequent contributor to the Evangelical Baptist Magazine as well as other periodicals. His first book "Between Two Women, A Stratford Story" is a memoir written in a humourous style and became a Canadian Best Seller. While he makes his readers smile, he does relate a serious story. The book is a picture of life as most Canadians lived it in the depression years and the epochal war years that followed.

The author's second book "Between Two Worlds, A Canadian Story" is the sequel and takes the reader into the life of the author as he worked his way through college, his romance with the girl of his dreams whom he married. This second book is a peek into the parsonage and the adventures of a typical Canadian minister. Pure Canadiana! It has no sermons but the story introduces us to many Canadians that remind us of the unsung heroes that have made the Northwest the amazing land that we call Canada. Rev. Woods lives in Ancaster, Ontario. He and his wife Joan have four married children with ten grandchildren. He is still available for speaking engagements and can be reached through email, brjwoods@cogeco.ca. Phone 905-648-1589